CONSUMER BEHAVIOR:
THEORY AND APPLICATIONS

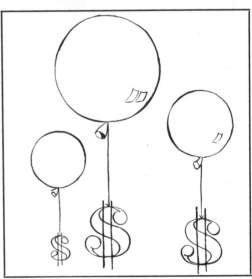

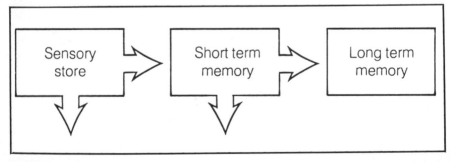

CONSUMER BEHAVIOR: THEORY AND APPLICATIONS

Barbara J. Redman, Ph.D.

Dept. of Agricultural Economics
University of Georgia

AVI PUBLISHING COMPANY, INC.
Westport, Connecticut

Library of Congress Cataloging in Publication Data

Redman, Barbara J.
    Consumer behavior

    Includes index.
    1. Consumers.   2.   Consumption (Economics)
I.   Title.
HB801.R37   658.8'34   79-16783
ISBN 0-87055-324-0

Printed in the United States of America

Preface

This book argues for the unity of the various social science disciplines. It focuses on consumer behavior as an aspect of human behavior, since all the disciplines considered have dealt with this particular area, although the concepts and frameworks used may apply to other forms of behavior as well. All the social sciences complement each other by specializing in areas of behavior, but they also all fit into the same general theoretical framework.

Economics has developed the most general and the most formal theory. This book will start from there and consider how the other disciplines contribute by developing further the simplifying assumptions which economics makes. At the same time, by broadening the traditional definitions of economic terms one can see how economic theory applies to a range of noneconomic phenomena.

For example, the budget line represents the information the consumer has about the situation, the costs of the alternatives and the resources the consumer has *as perceived by the consumer*. Here the psychological theories of perception enter to analyze the reasons why consumers when confronted with the same body of information may retain different impressions of it. As consumers can only act on the basis of information which they have, this may help explain some seemingly "irrational" decisions.

The question of rationality itself becomes moot in the definition of the motivational assumption of utility maximization.

Each person will seek to maximize his/her own satisfaction as he/she perceives it at the time of decision. What constitutes satisfaction for a person may vary; here enter the motivation theorists. Differences in perception have already been noted. We then can turn to the individual's preferences.

An individual's preferences, as shown in the indifference map, can reflect the individual's attitudes (if one uses a cognitive approach) or response sets (if one takes a behaviorist approach). One can then begin discussions on the structure and function of attitudes and the empirical findings by the social psychologists on the relationship of attitudes to behavior.

Two major types of factors influence attitudes: the individual's personality (factors within the individual) and social influence on the individual (factors external to the individual). As many views on personality exist, several of the major theorists and evidence linking these theories to consumption behavior are presented. Conformity to a reference group is discussed as the process through which social influence operates on a person. The major types of reference groups we observe in consumer behavior are an individual's social class and culture. Discussion of the family as a reference group is deferred until a later chapter.

The above factors describe the determinants of a person's present choice. However, present choices have repercussions on future attitudes, perceptions and choices. Attitude, learning and perceptual changes are considered as the forms in which these repercussions occur.

Finally, as an example of parallel development of economic and social psychological theory, exchange theory is described. Since the family may at times operate as a reference group and at other times a bargaining unit, exchange and consumption decisions within the family serve as an illustration of this theory.

A few major ideas will run through all the theories considered. First, all presume and some explicitly state a person's need for organization and consistency. Perception, attitude and some personality theories especially emphasize this; economics assumes consistent preferences. Second, a principle of diminishing returns, at least, and perhaps the more general law of variable proportions, seems to operate for a variety of phenomena. The physical principle is well established in economic production theory and it also appears to hold psychologically.

The older marginal utility theory involves the assumption of diminishing marginal utility; indifference curve analysis assumes a diminishing marginal rate of substitution. One can also observe this in the physiological areas of psychology. For example, the effects of physiological arousal and time spent learning follow the same pattern of diminishing returns with respect to performance. While personality theories have not explicitly included this principle, most imply that a person will pursue a diverse range of activities, which is one consequence of diminishing returns. Maslow in his motivation theory, by stating that as one level of needs is satisfied another becomes dominant, makes use of this idea. If diminishing returns did not hold, a person could continue to gratify one need indefinitely and never concern him/herself with the others.

A third continual theme in these theories is a structural one concerning desires versus situational constraints on desires. A person, in acting, must consider not only his/her own preferences but also the situation and the limits he/she faces in the situation. Economic theory has the indifference curve/budget line interaction; attitude theory incorporates both an attitude toward an object and an attitude toward the situation. Most personality theories focus on the person's development within the constraints of the person's environment.

A final universal theme concerns the person's motivation. All theories share the economic assumption that the person will act so as to maximize his/her satisfaction subject to existing constraints. This directly relates to the third theme. The theories differ on precisely what that means, that is, the form which the maximization of satisfaction will take. Also, different labels are used. For example, attitudinal consistency theorists speak of dissonance reduction and learning theorists speak of tension reduction. The reduction of unpleasantness is the other side of the enhancement of pleasure.

These themes could be considered as major general laws of human behavior. Most of the various theories rest on slightly differing interpretations and contexts of these laws and on varying definitions of the terms involved.

This book differs from any other book I have seen in that I have tried to actually integrate the various theories without recourse to a systems approach (which to me seems to be descriptive rather than explanatory). Further, I have done this from an economic perspective, in contrast to most books on consumer behavior which either omit all mention of the economic theory of consumer choice or briefly mention marginal utility theory as an historical relic. In fact, this contrast is so far true that I am not sure that there exist any truly close competitors.

I intend this book for two audiences. First, I developed it for use in a one-semester, three-credit hour, upper-level undergraduate course in consumer behavior which has a prerequisite of the introductory courses in the social sciences, although not all students need to have this background. I have taught a course for several years lecturing from this book and am satisfied with the organization of the material. I have included practical applications written by former students and selected references at the end of each chapter in order to illustrate theories and provide the student with information for further research.

Second, I intend this book for professional economists. Most economists have little or no appreciation of the other social sciences; some dimly recognize that psychosociological factors influence consumer choice, but few have any knowledge of these factors. This book should serve as an introduction for economists to the world of behavioral science, especially since it fits into the economist's existing mind-set of indifference-curve analysis.

This author also wishes to express her appreciation to Dr. Norman W. Desrosier, Ms. Lisa E. Melilli and the AVI Publishing Company for encouragement and assistance in bringing this book into being.

I have tried to provide a fairly concise overview, again with an interest in retaining the integrative flow of thought. As such, I hope this book will facilitate cross-discipline interaction.

BARBARA J. REDMAN, Ph. D.

March 1979

Contributors

BARGESKI, DEBRA J. 4005 Holly Tree Rd., Marlow Heights, Md. 20031

BURTON, KATHLEEN S. 629 Breton Place, Arnold, Md. 21012

CARUS, RUTH F. 1516 Shadyside, Baltimore, Md. 21218

CUNNINGHAM, DORIS H. 2204 Hermitage Ave., Silver Spring, Md. 20902

DALRYMPLE, ELZORA M. 7415 Holly Ave., Takoma Park, Md. 20012

HERONDORF, BARBARA A. 6217 Fernwood Terr. 202, Riverdale, Md. 20840

KICKERT, MELANIE R. 2020 Hillyer Pl., N.W., Washington, D.C. 20009

MURPHY, JOHN S. 4419 Puller Dr., Kensington, Md. 20795

SELSOR, KAREN P. 1303 Oakcrest Dr., Alexandria, Va. 22302

SHIEH, GRACE A. 11201 Woodlawn Blvd., Upper Marlboro, Md. 20870

SILLS, DAVID M. 5025 53rd Place, Hyattsville, Md. 20781

WILDENSTEINER, LINDA K. 6203 Belwood Street, District Heights, Md. 20028

Table of Contents

PREFACE
1 A Theory of Consumer Behavior:
  Methodological Foundations   1
2 The Economic Framework for Choice   14
3 Broadening the Economic Concepts   43
4 Indifference Curves: Attitudes/
  Response Sets   74
5 Factors Affecting Attitudes:
  Personality   88
6 Factors Affecting Attitudes:
  Social Influence   118
7 After the Choice: Modifications of
  Attitude/Response Sets/Perceptions   145
8 Exchange Theory in Economics and
  Social Psychology   185
9 General Laws Revisited   217
  INDEX   221

1

A Theory of Consumer Behavior: Methodological Foundations

All the words in the title of this chapter, *A Theory of Consumer Behavior*, carry significance. First of all, the emphasis is on theory rather than application, although applications will illustrate the theory. Applications change with every new government pronouncement and national crisis, but theories (we hope) retain their validity throughout changing circumstances. The emphasis is also on explanation rather than description of a phenomena. Ultimate understanding comes through answers to *why?*, not through answers to *how?* Again, the *why* answers to one phenomenon may generalize to another, while the *how* answers do so far less readily. As a result, a deductive approach rather than a simulation approach will be used.

This book entails *a* theory. Although many different theories from several disciplines will be used, although mainly economics and psychology, the argument will be that these are merely different aspects of a single, more general theory. It is not claimed this is *the* theory which rules out other perspectives.

This theory is of human behavior and will focus on consumer behavior. Under the traditional narrow definition regarding consumption of physical goods and services, one may consider consumer behavior as an application of the more general theory. Under a broader definition, one could argue that in all activities we are in fact consumers of something, whether or not the *something* is a tangible good. Under this viewpoint, consumer behavior subsumes other areas of behavior.

First, some philosophical justification is in order for the adoption of a unified perspective. One could question both the unity of the social sciences and the possibility of any kind of theory in any of them, since social science deals with individuals who have independence of thought and action. The logical procedure then would be to start at the most basic level with the nature of a theory.

THE CONSTRUCTION OF A THEORY

A theory is an explanation of why an event has occurred. A theoretical system is a collection of theoretical statements related to, describing and explaining the same class of phenomena.

Theories consist of axioms, which are fundamental assumptions of the theory, and theorems. Theorems are derived from the axioms; some theorems refer more or less directly to observable experience, while other theorems do not. Axioms should be independent, consistent and complete; completeness includes practicality and theoreticality. If axioms are not independent, one could obtain the same conclusion with a fewer number of them. Deriving theorems from independent axioms is analogous to solving a set of linearly independent equations, except that extra axioms are usually merely extraneous. In any theoretical system it is desirable to keep the number of axioms to a minimum so as to increase the cohesiveness and the explanatory power of the system.

Occam's Razor, which gives preference to theories containing the weakest and smallest set of assumptions, illustrates this point. Inconsistent axioms lead to contradictory conclusions. These need no further explanation. An incomplete set of axioms leaves a body of data which cannot be explained by the system. Completeness requires that axioms have some practical aspect so as to be applicable and be theoretical in order to have sufficient generality to cover the entire class of explainable phenomena.

Axioms and theorems are cast in the form of theoretical statements. A theoretical statement is composed of observable and theoretical terms. Observable terms refer to more or less directly ascertainable entities. Dispositional terms, a subset of the unobservable theoretical terms, refer to unobservable properties of observable entities. Purely theoretical terms refer to unobservable properties of unobservable entities.

Terms are placed together to make a theoretical statement, and theoretical statements to make a theory, by means of syntax, semantics and pragmatics (Rudner 1966). The following scheme illustrates the composition of these elements in a formal deductive system.

(A) Syntax: formalism, logic of use. Consists of
  (1) vocabulary: symbols that are employed, and
  (2) grammar: rules for use of symbols. Consists of
    (a) formation rules: rules of conventional English and jargon;
    (b) transformation rules: rules of inference, such as deductive logic.
(B) Semantics: interpretation. Consists of
  (1) primitives (undefined terms), distinguished from defined terms;
  (2) defined terms which are
    (a) full definitions, which establish synonymical relations between expressions, and partial definitions, which specify only in part or indirectly the meaning of a term or expression; or
    (b) nominal definitions, arbitrarily specified, and real definitions, which indicate essential characteristics; and
  (3) correspondence rules: rules which connect theoretical terms with possible observations.

The formalism and interpretation comprise a scientific theory which then needs data on which to build.

For example, consider the statement in economics of the law of variable proportions, in a rather unelaborate form: "As the amount of a variable input is increased, the amount of other (fixed) inputs held constant, the rate of increase of output relative to that of the variable input is first positive and increasing, then positive and decreasing, and eventually negative."

In this statement, the syntax seems fairly obvious. The symbols employed consist of words and are connected according to rules of grammar. Primitive terms are "input" and "output." "Rate of increase of output," still a theoretical term, will be defined by the statement in real terms, as the sign and degree of change denote essential characteristics. This would comprise a full definition as it indicates a sequential order of all possibilities. One could further nominally define, for example, labor as input and product X as output and thus deduce (transformation rule) a statement about the production of the product X. Observable terms in the statement are "amount" and "rate." One could find rules of correspondence, such as standards of measurement, to connect "amount" and "rate" with "input" and "output." "Increase," "decrease," "relative," "positive" and "negative" also help relate the two classes of terms.

THE NATURE OF EXPLANATION

The formulation of any theoretical system involves deductive and inductive logic. Most theories are discovered inductively and formulated and tested deductively. Inductive reasoning involves the following: (1) observation of the subject matter the theory is meant to explain, (2) classification of the observed data into assorted groupings during which the researcher speculates on a plausible hypothesis, and (3) generalization made about the data or adoption of the most probable hypothesis.

Theoretical statements found in this way must then be tested. A researcher first obtains an implication of the statement, frequently by expecting a general statement to hold for a specific case, then empirically confirms or disconfirms the implication. If the implication is true, the theoretical hypothesis has received added support but cannot be absolutely confirmed as the chance exists that the next test may prove it false. If the implication is false and it is a logical deductive consequence of the hypothesis, then the hypothesis must be false. In deductive logic the premises of a line of reasoning contain the conclusion, such as "if A then B, and A exists, therefore B exists." If B does not exist, then either A does not exist or it is not true that "if A then B." If the premises of a deductive argument are true, then the conclusion must be true; if the conclusion is false, at least one of the premises must be false. Deductive reasoning is infallible. Most debate over theories centers on whether the premises are true or appropriate and on the numerous conditions which often are assumed constant.

Several philosophers in this area, most notably Carl Hempel (1952), contend that deductive logic, with at least one of the premises a general law and the others antecedent conditions to the laws, either explicitly or implicitly comprises the basis of all adequate scientific or rational explanation and prediction. In a deductive model, explanation and prediction are entirely symmetrical. In explaining how an event happened, one consciously or unconsciously assumes that a general law exists which covers the situation and from which one could deduce or predict this event. For example:

General law: All lumps of sugar when put into hot teas dissolve.

Antecedent condition: This lump of sugar was put into hot tea.

Conclusion: This lump of sugar dissolved.

One can obtain theoretical systems in this way as one can ultimately deduce each general law from another more general one. Samuelson (1964) also makes this point, however, he fails to recognize the procedure as an explanation in itself even though it may not be the ultimate explanation. Each statement consists of a description; the syllogism comprises explanation. The deductive explanatory process could conceivably go on forever, but due to limits on human knowledge, one always postulates general laws at the point where one cannot infer further. These become axioms of the system.

Hempel stated four conditions for the explanation to be adequate:

(1) the conclusion must be logically deductible from the premises;

(2) the premises must contain general laws that are actually required for deriving the conclusion;

(3) the premises must be capable, at least in principle, of test by experiment or observation; and

(4) the premises must be true.

Because one cannot actually prove a statement, since the chance always exists that the next trial may negate it, the fourth condition is usually interpreted as requiring a high degree of confirmation. Where the premises are only probable, the conclusion has only the probability of the premises.

APPLICABILITY TO SOCIAL SCIENCES: SOME CONSIDERATIONS

Hempel originally intended his covering law model to apply to the physical sciences. Economics and psychology, in particular, use the same methodology for studying both physical and non-physical phenomena. Many have wondered if this is justified, since social science deals with human behavior which one cannot expect to function as regularly and predictably as physical objects and processes.

An Inexact Science

John Stuart Mill (1876) was one of the earliest social scientists, as such, to question the possibility of social science. He concluded that social science was an inexact science in that one could never know all of the relevant factors involved in a person's behavior and that no two people would ever have the exact same motives or react in exactly the same manner. Even so, one could identify general trends of behavior and make general predictions which would almost always be verified; "an approximate generalization is, in social inquiries, for most practical purposes equivalent to an exact one: that which is only probable when asserted of individual human beings indiscriminately selected, being certain when affirmed of the character and collective conduct of masses." Mill also recommended that to give a genuinely scientific character to social science, the approximate generalizations should be shown as logically deducible from universal laws of human nature and that from these deductions other generalizations may be deduced. Hempel's position strongly resembles Mill's on this point.

Fritz Machlup (1961) examined in detail nine of the grounds most often cited in comparing social and physical science: invariability of observations, objectivity of observations and explanations, verifiability of hypotheses, exactness of findings, measurability of phenomena, constancy of numerical relationships, predictability of future events, distance from everyday experience, and standards of admissions and requirements. He did not consider the last two relevant to the nature of the disciplines in judging inferiority. Of the remainder, only on "invariance," "verifiability" and "numerical constants" did social science emerge inferior to natural science. Machlup concluded that the only difference indicated was that social science studies different kinds of phenomena from natural science and, although less exact, is no less of a science.

Individual vs Society

Another question raised in studying social science concerns whether the individuals, acting separately, determine their culture and sociopolitical institutions, or whether they are molded by cultural forces so as to yield fairly uniform behavior. Economics tends to regard the individual as the basis for economic institutions; psychology and sociology focus more on how the individual is shaped by the social environment.

This question seems to boil down to the chicken-or-the-egg argument: does the individual produce the culture or the culture produce the individual? The same people who would argue for the chicken (via Creation) would probably claim that humans came first and shaped their own culture through interaction. The origin of both chicken-and-egg and individual-and-culture is now irrelevant, though, since we are now in the midst of the process. In both cases, the whole system (poultry or civilization) is evolving through time.

It seems obvious that neither factor (individual or culture) has complete dominance. If the individual were completely shaped by culture, all individuals would behave in the same way and there would be no social change. However, a great deal of social change and widely differing individual behavior frequently occur, so therefore, culture-as-sole determinant will not work satisfactorily. On the other hand, if the individuals acting separately determined the social institutions and were not in any way influenced by them, their descendants would act entirely differently and no lasting regularities could be observed. This is not the case either.

Obviously these are extreme oversimplifications. Bronislaw Malinowski (1944) claims that organization came about in response to basic human biological needs which had to be satisfied. Once the organization was established, however, it became as vital and compelling as the original biological needs since it satisfied those needs. Organization may change only to fulfill a new need, which arises out of the organization. He does not specify how this happens.

Even J. W. N. Watkins (1953) who is the leading proponent of "methodological individualism," which holds that individuals are the basis for and the actors in all social action and institutions and social phenomena do not create themselves, separates dispositions of individuals into two kinds. These are private and temperamental ones, and public and institutional ones. The latter provide the social scientists with subject matter sufficiently stable to form generalizations. Watkins does not object to theories of social phenomena or even oversimplified versions (ideal types) so long as they make clear that the social phenomena result from individual interaction.

Limitations on Theories in Social Science

Since the public dispositions comprise only part of an individual's character and personality quirks affect his/her actions, the generalizations based on the public dispositions are of necessity ideal types. If the generalizations are stated as laws, they become ceteris paribus laws, holding the private dispositions constant. If one could determine a person's private interpretation of a stimulus to behavior and knew the general laws, one could precisely predict his/her actions.

The ideal types, or explanations in principle, also assume that everyone always acts rationally in the way commonly identified. Rationality is also divided into two types: rationality of belief and rationality of action (Watkins 1953). Rationality of belief is drawing appropriate conclusions on the basis of relevant evidence. Rationality of action is acting in accordance with one's beliefs and motives, even if these are irrational of belief. Ideal types assume that rationality of belief is the same for everyone and as a consequence everyone acts rationally in the same way, as it is generally assumed that all individuals are rational of action. Ideal types as such cannot explain "irrational" or unconventional behavior. For this, explanation in detail is needed which psychology frequently provides. Although the simplifying assumptions somewhat weaken the deductive system, since a false conclusion could result from the inadequacy of one of these assumptions, the covering law model still applies to ideal types.

The use of ceteris paribus complicates application of a theory in prediction as well as in explanation. A decision must be made on how much of assumed ceteris paribus in one law is relevant to a situation and should be accounted for by another law. It is also possible for two laws under a conjunction of conditions to work in opposite directions and leave the result indeterminate, for example, if a consumer's income and the prices he/she faces both increase. In all of these cases a decision is usually made on the basis of background knowledge of the situation which not everyone has. This is where experts play a role in theory (Helmer and Rescher 1959).

TESTABILITY OF A THEORY

Much debate also has taken place over whether the premises of an argument must be true or even testable (Melitz 1965). In Hempel's model, the premises must be testable by the very nature of the argument. If the premises contain the conclusion and the conclusion is assumed to descibe some empirical phenomenon, then the premises must contain potentially observable elements and describe empirical phenomena. Therefore, the premises can be tested, at least in principle, although it may be that no one as yet has had the tools or resources to test them. While definitions cannot be tested in themselves, they can be tested for their appropriateness to the situation which the assumptions implicitly involve. For example, economists frequently use variables like "profit," "cost," "price," etc., as proxies for a wider range of nonmonetary benefits and costs because of practical convenience. Clearly, this is not always appropriate.

It has also been suggested (Machlup 1955) that certain principles are in fact rules and not laws, and as such do not need verification. Social rules differ from natural laws on three counts:

(1) Rules are neither true nor false. They simply exist.
(2) Laws are empirically rooted and cannot be violated even deliberately, while rules are normative and require voluntary or forced compliance to be effective.
(3) Rules as social conventions are subject to change, while laws are structural principles of nature.

If economic principles are indeed rules, then they do not need verification since rules are neither true nor false, but neither does ground-work exist for any kind of theory if rules may change at any time. One could argue that many of the economic behavioral theorists' premises (such as satisficing and rule-of-thumb price markups) and many of the sociological delineations (such as social class and inequality) are in fact rules, which as such are subject to change and are not foundations of a theory. By the same reasoning, computer simulation techniques can test descriptions but not theories.

A premise may be untrue in three ways: (1) it may be an incomplete description of reality (almost any premise is guilty of this), (2) it may be contrary to observed facts, or (3) it may be an abstraction from reality as an ideal type (Nagel 1963). The third has been previously discussed.

If a premise is false in the sense of being contrary to facts, it can yield misleading results in two ways. If it is used in generating a law, or it is the law and the law is false, the conclusion may by chance be true but no guarantee exists that the law will continue to yield correct conclusions. If the false premise is an antecedent condition, a false conclusion could be attributed to either the condition or to the law being used. A tendency to assign all the blame to the condition may result in the acceptance and use of false laws. The closer the conditions approach reality, the less chance that any error will lie in the conditions and the more confidence one can feel in the general law (Melitz 1965). Therefore, empirical work plays an important role in the testing of theories as well as in the discovery of new hypotheses.

SOME GENERAL LAWS OF HUMAN BEHAVIOR

The foregoing discussion should lay a methodological foundation for the unity of the various social science disciplines which will be argued in the pages to come. The focus will be on consumer behavior as an aspect of human behavior. It will be argued that all the social sciences complement each other by specializing in areas of behavior, but they also all fit into the same general theoretical framework. Economics has developed the most general and the most formal theory. This approach will start from there and consider how the other disciplines contribute by developing further the simplifying assumptions which economics makes. At the same time, by broadening the traditional definitions of economic terms one can see how economic theory applies to a range of noneconomic phenomena. Not only the terms involved, but also the term "consumer" may be taken in a very broad sense. As mentioned earlier, one could argue that in every action taken, an individual consumes something and at some cost. This will be elaborated upon later.

A few major ideas will run through all the theories considered. First, all presume and some explicitly state a person's need of organization and consistency. Perception, attitude and some personality theories especially emphasize this; economics assumes consistent preferences.

Second, a principle of diminishing returns, at least, and perhaps the more general law of variable proportions, seems to operate for a variety of phenomena. The physical principle is well established in economic production theory and it also appears to hold psychologically. The older marginal utility theory involves the assumption of diminishing marginal utility; indifference curve analysis assumes a diminishing marginal rate of substitution. One can also observe this in the physiological areas of psychology. For example, the effects of physiological arousal and time spent learning follow the same pattern of diminishing returns with respect to performance. While personality theories have not explicitly included this principle, most imply that a person will pursue a diverse range of activities, which is one consequence of diminishing returns. Maslow, by stating that as one level of needs is satisfied another becomes dominant, makes use of this idea. If diminishing returns did not hold, a person could continue to gratify one need indefinitely and never concern him/herself with the others.

A third continual theme in these theories, and one which will be emphasized in the following analysis, is a structural one concerning desires versus situational constraints on desires. A person, in acting, must consider not only his/her own preferences but also the situation and the limits he/she faces in the situation. Economic theory has the indifference curve/budget line interaction; attitude theory incorporates both an attitude toward an object and an attitude toward the situation. Most personality theories focus on the person's development within the constraints of the person's environment.

A final universal theme concerns the person's motivation. All theories share the economic assumption that the person will act so as to maximize his/her satisfaction subject to existing constraints. This directly relates to the third theme. They differ on precisely what that means, that is, the form which the maximization of satisfaction will take. Also, different labels are used. For example, attitudinal consistency theorists speak of dissonance reduction and learning theorists speak of tension reduction. The reduction of unpleasantness is the other side of the enhancement of pleasure.

These themes could be considered as major general laws of human behavior. Most of the various theories rest on slightly differing interpretations and contexts of these laws and on varying definitions of the terms involved.

REFERENCES

FRIEDMAN, M. 1948. The methodology of positive economics. *In* Essays in Positive Economics. Univ. of Chicago Press, Chicago.

HELMER, O. and RESCHER, N. 1959. On the epistemology of the inexact science. Manag. Sci. *6*, 25-52.

HEMPEL, C. 1952. Fundamentals of Concept Formation in Empirical Science. Univ. of Chicago Press, Chicago.

HEMPEL, C. and OPPENHEIM, P. 1969. The logic of explanation. *In* The Nature and Scope of Social Science: A Critical Anthology (L. Krimerman, Editor.) Appleton-Century-Crofts, New York.

MACHLUP, F. 1955. The problem of verification in economics. Southern Econ. J. *21*, 1-21.

MACHLUP, F. 1961. Are the social sciences really inferior? Southern Econ. J. *27*, 173-184.

MACHLUP, F. 1964. Professor Samuelson on theory and realism. Amer. Econ. Rev. *54*, 733-735.

MALINOWSKI, B. 1944. A Scientific Theory of Culture. Univ. of North Carolina Press, Chapel Hill.

MELITZ, J. 1965. Friedman and Machlup on the significance of testing economic assumption. J. Polit. Econ. *73*, 37-60.

MILL, J. 1876. A System of Logic. Longman's Green and Co., London.

NAGEL, E. 1963. Assumptions in economic theory. Amer. Econ. Rev. *53*, 211-219.

REDMAN, B. 1976. On economic theory and explanation. J. Behavioral Econ. *5*, 160-176.

RUDNER, R. 1966. Philosophy of Social Science. Prentice-Hall, Englewood Cliffs, N.J.

SAMUELSON, P. 1963. Problems of methodology-discussion. Amer. Econ. Rev. *53*, 231-236.

SAMUELSON, P. 1964. Theory and realism: A reply. Amer. Econ. Rev. *54*, 733-735.

WATKINS, J. 1953. Ideal types and historical explanation. *In* Readings in the Philosophy of Science (Feigl and Brodbeck, Editors.) Appleton-Century-Crofts, New York.

The Economic Framework for Choice

2

The basic simplifying assumptions made in economic demand theory are that (1) the consumer is aware of the existence of some goods and services, (2) the consumer has some preferences among these goods and services, and (3) the consumer has some money income in order for these preferences to affect his/her spending behavior. More restrictive assumptions, such as that of complete information on all relevant matters, are unnecessary for consumer choice; the consumer will act on the basis of the information he/she has. For motivation, economic theory assumes the consumer maximizes his/her satisfaction subject to market constraints. One can make further assumptions on consumer preferences, depending upon the approach which one uses.

MARGINAL UTILITY ANALYSIS

The older marginal utility approach no longer appears in research literature, but it does give an intuitive grasp of the concepts and processes. All versions of demand theory presume that the consumer (or consuming unit) derives a certain amount of satisfaction (or utility) from each good or service he/she consumes in a given time period. Marginal utility theory assumes that (1) this amount of satisfaction is somehow measurable, and (2) this total amount of satisfaction increases at a decreasing rate with the quantity of the good consumed. Alternatively stated, the marginal utility of the good (the extra satisfaction derived from an extra unit of the good) decreases as the quantity consumed increases. For example, a person drinking beer would not get as much of an increase in satisfaction from the seventh beer as he/she would from the first, and less extra satisfaction from the tenth than from the seventh. If the person drank so much that he/she became sick, at that point an extra beer would decrease the person's total utility. This roughly follows the law of variable proportions mentioned earlier (the first segment of the curve is questionable).

All economic theory assumes that the person maximizes his/her total utility. In marginal utility theory, with the additional assumption that the utility derived from one good is independent of the utility derived from another good, one could show that the consumer can maximize his/her total utility by allocating his/her income among various goods so that:

$$\frac{MU_x}{P_x} = \frac{MU_y}{P_y} = \frac{MU_z}{P_z} = \ldots$$

where x, y and z are goods, MU_x refers to the extra satisfaction (marginal utility) derived from the last unit of good X, P_x is the price of good X, etc. Alternatively stated, the marginal utilities of the last dollar spent on each good are equal.

The problem with the use of the marginal utility approach rests with its reliance on the measurability of levels of utility. The tools with which to obtain an absolute standard of total utility simply do not exist. Conceivably, such tools could eventually be developed but their present absence renders the entire marginal utility theory impotent.

INDIFFERENCE CURVE ANALYSIS

Indifference curve analysis, the theory of consumer choice presently used by economists, breaks with marginal utility theory by relying on ordinal, rather than cardinal measurement of utility. Ordinal utility refers to the ordering of preferences rather than measurement of the absolute level of satisfaction which they bring.

Preferences: Indifference Curves

Indifference curve analysis involves four additional assumptions to the list previously mentioned on consumer preferences.

(1) For any two combinations A and B of goods, a consumer either prefers A to B, B to A, or is indifferent between them.
(2) The consumer's preferences will be consistent and transitive. If he/she prefers A to B and B to C, he/she will prefer A to C.
(3) The consumer will always prefer more of a good to less of it, assuming quantities of other goods are constant.
(4) The consumer's preferences will reflect a diminishing marginal rate of substitution. The consumer more highly values an extra unit of the good of which he/she has but relatively little, and this higher valuation results in willingness to give up relatively more of another good in order to obtain it. This is very similar to the concept of diminishing marginal utility.

Since the consumer can rank combinations of goods in order of preference, he/she will prefer some combinations to others. Still others would give the consumer the same amount of satisfaction, so the consumer is indifferent between them. In Fig. 2.1, the locus of the combinations of goods X and Y among which the consumer is indifferent constitutes an indifference curve. The further northeast the indifference curve lies on the graph, the higher level of satisfaction it represents since it reflects more of both goods than does a lower indifference curve, and by assumption more is preferred to less.

Some characteristics of indifference curves which result from the assumptions made include a downward slope and concavity from above (from the assumption of diminishing rate of marginal

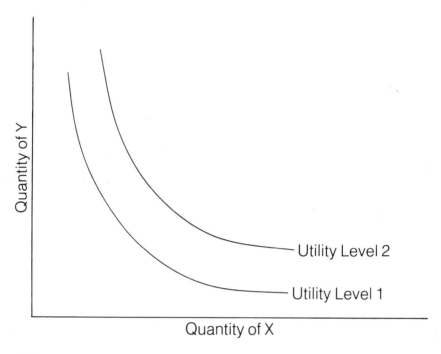

FIG. 2.1.   UTILITY SURFACE OF A CONSUMER

substitution),[1] nonintersection (from transitivity and more pre-ferred to less)[2] and an infinite number of them in space. Their slopes reflect the relative preferences of a consumer among the goods on the axes. The consumer may have a strong preference for good X; the consumer would be willing to give up a lot of Y to obtain a little more of X (Fig. 2.2A). On the other hand the consumer may have a strong preference for Y; the consumer

---

[1] If the consumer can exchange some of one good for another good and retain the orginal level of satisfaction, the indifference curve slopes downward. If the person has relatively little of Y already, and as such requires greater X to compensate for a further sacrifice of Y than if the person had originally had a large amount of Y, the curve is concave from above.

[2] If two indifference curves intersect, an inconsistency arises. A higher indifference curve indicates greater satisfaction, but in the case of inter-section a curve is for some choices higher and for other choices lower than another curve. Since points on an indifference curve reflect equal satisfac-tion, this means that in some cases a greater quantity of both goods is considered inferior to a lesser quantity, which violates assumption 3.

requires a lot of X to compensate for the loss of a little Y (or conversely would give up a lot of X for a little more Y) (Fig. 2.2B).

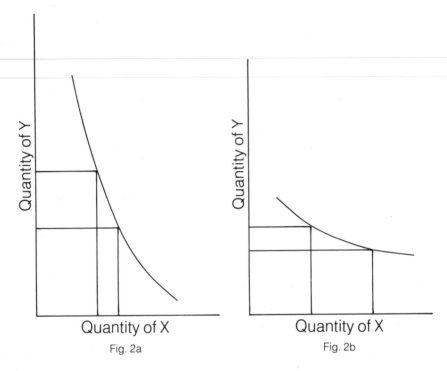

Fig. 2a

Fig. 2b

FIG. 2.2.   RELATIVE PREFERENCES OF A CONSUMER BETWEEN TWO GOODS

In short, the indifference curves reflect the consumer's preferences or what the consumer would *like* to do. This is independent of what is *possible* to do which is shown in the budget line.

Possibilities: Budget Lines

The consumer has a limited amount of money income, M, (from any source, not necessarily wages). If two goods are available, the consumer may spend this income on either good or some combination of the two. Price per unit of a good times the number of units purchased determines the amount spent on a good. The amount spent on the goods cannot exceed the amount of money the consumer has. Borrowing merely increases the amount the consumer has to spend. Therefore, the budget equation becomes $P_x X + P_y Y \leq M$, where P_x and P_y represent prices per unit of X and Y, respectively. In graphing the range of possibilities (Fig. 2.3), one may graph the equality

$$M = P_x X + P_y Y, \text{ or } Y = \frac{1}{P_y} M - \frac{P_x}{P_y} X.$$

where $\frac{M}{P_y}$ represents the intercept of the line, and $-\frac{P_x}{P_y}$, the rate of relative prices, its slope. With income and prices constant, one must give up some of X to obtain more of Y.

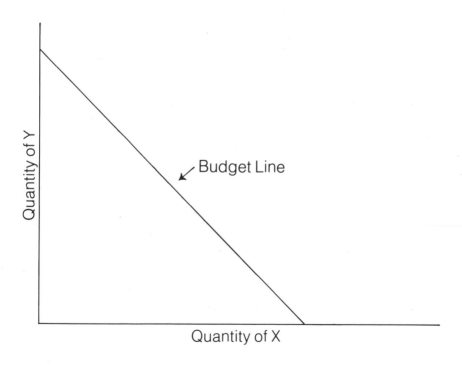

FIG. 2.3.   A CONSUMER'S BUDGET LINE

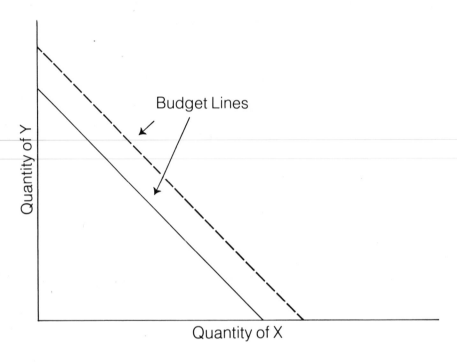

Budget Lines

Quantity of Y

Quantity of X

FIG. 2.4.   A SHIFT OF BUDGET LINE WITH INCREASED INCOME

As the budget line depends on income and prices, changes in either will shift the line. A change in income, affecting the intercept, will cause a parallel shift of the line—outward for an income increase (Fig. 2.4) and inward for a decrease (Fig. 2.5). With an increase in available resources, one could purchase more of either or both goods. The opposite holds for a decrease in available resources. An increase in the price of X relative to the price of Y (assume for simplicity the price of Y is unchanged) will result in a steeper sloped line (Fig. 2.6). The total amount of Y one could buy if one spent all one's income on Y does not change. If one spent the total income on X, one could now buy fewer units of X, since the price of each X increased. Thus, with a price (of X) increase and with the axes labeled as above, the budget line will rotate inward. Similarly, a decrease in the price of X means that while the amount of Y one could obtain if one bought only Y remains constant, the amount of X one could buy if one bought only X has increased (Fig. 2.7). Therefore, the budget line rotates outward in this case.

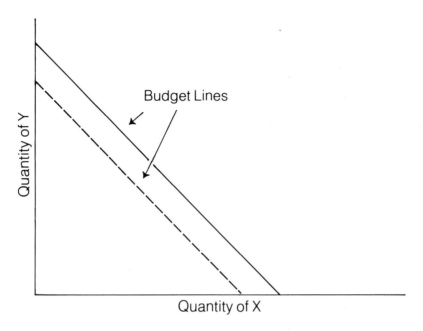

FIG. 2.5.   A SHIFT OF BUDGET LINE WITH DECREASED INCOME

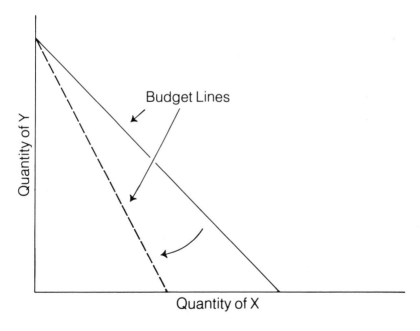

FIG. 2.6.   BUDGET LINES WITH INCREASE IN PRICE OF X

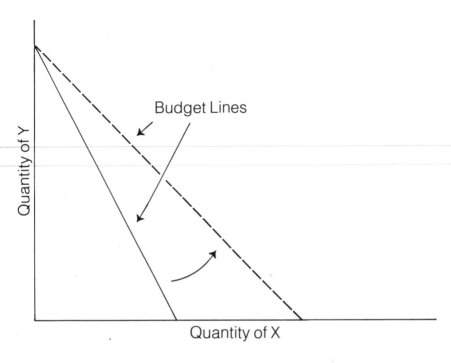

FIG. 2.7.   BUDGET LINES WITH DECREASE IN PRICE OF X

The Choice

With information on the consumer's own preferences and on the situation (market) constraints on these preferences, the consumer will choose among the alternative goods so as to maximize his/her satisfaction subject to these constraints. Of all the possible choices, the consumer will choose that which he/she prefers most. Graphically, this happens at the point where the budget line is tangent to the highest possible indifference curve (Fig. 2.8, point A). Any other point (such as B) on the budget line lies on a lower indifference curve and as such will not be chosen. The choice of point A implies the consumption of quantity X_1 of good X and quantity Y_1 of good Y.

The consumer's choice process operates in this fashion for a given set of preferences and possibilities. As the possibilities change, the choice will change but continues to be made according to the above criterion. One can trace the pattern of choices for given changes in income and prices.

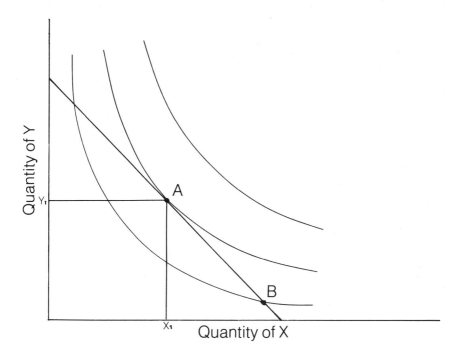

FIG. 2.8.   A CONSUMER'S SET OF INDIFFERENCE CURVES

Change In Income

Consider the effects of changes in income, with relative prices constant (Fig. 2.9). Suppose the consumer originally had income as represented by the lowest budget line and as such chose the combination point A (X_1 and Y_1). If the consumer's income increases (shown by the next higher budget line), point A no longer represents the choice of the greatest possible satisfaction. It is now possible to obtain more of both goods, which by assumption would increase satisfaction. The consumer is thus faced with a new range of possibilities, from which to choose the most preferred. The same process operates as with the first budget line; the new choice will be point B (X_2 and Y_2). Similarly, a further increase in income (shown by the highest budget line) results in the choice point C (X_3 and Y_3). A line connecting all of these points represents the combination of X and Y chosen at differing levels of income and is known as the income-consumption curve.

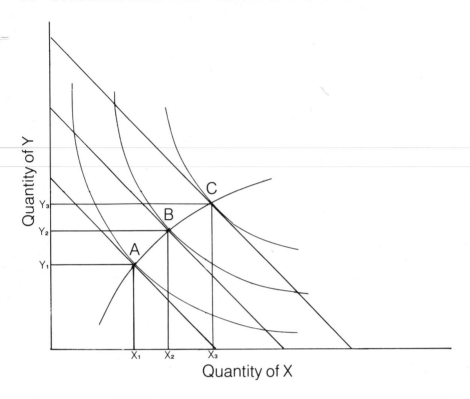

FIG. 2.9.   THE EFFECT OF CHANGES IN INCOME WITH PRICES CONSTANT

One can also relate the consumption of a good directly to the amount of the consumer's income (Fig. 2.10). Let M_1, M_2, M_3 represent the levels of income reflected in the three budget lines of Fig. 2.9. X_1, X_2 and X_3 are the same as in Fig. 2.9. The line connecting the resulting points is known as an Engel curve. One could also obtain from Fig. 2.9 an Engel curve for good Y (see Fig. 2.11).

Engel curves may take any of three basic shapes. A curve like Fig. 2.10 implies that income could change even a small amount and the amount of X consumed would change considerably. Goods such as X, "superior goods," tend to be luxury types of goods. A curve like Fig. 2.11 indicates that income could change quite a bit with little impact on the consumption of Y. This kind of good, termed a "normal good," tends to be a necessity. For example, since a person requires a certain amount of food and since stomach capacity is not limitless, a person's food consumption should not change drastically as income changes. The third

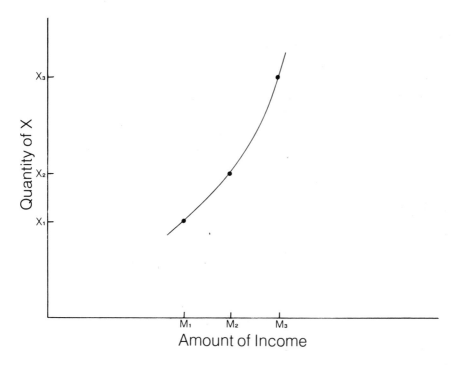

FIG. 2.10.   AN ENGEL CURVE FOR GOOD X

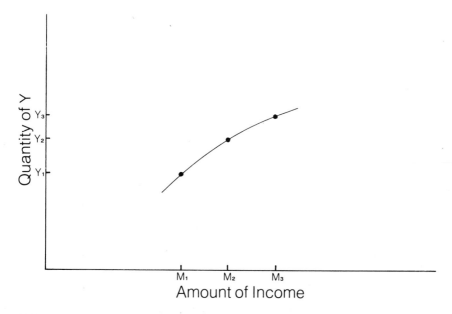

FIG. 2.11.   AN ENGEL CURVE FOR GOOD Y

possibility is a downward-sloped curve as in Fig. 2.12. One may obtain this from an indifference-curve diagram by carefully drawing the curves. The consumption of good Z, termed an "inferior good," decreases as income increases. Goods of this type are not common. The classic example used to be margarine, which in its early years was a less expensive, lower quality substitute for butter. As incomes rose, people switched to butter which they could then afford and therefore consumed less margarine.

Change In Prices

Effects on choice of changes in relative prices, with money income constant, can also be traced (Fig. 2.13). Consider a price increase for good X. Suppose the original price of X is that indicated by the highest budget line. Point A implies the consumption of X_1 of X and Y_1 of Y. If the price of X now increases

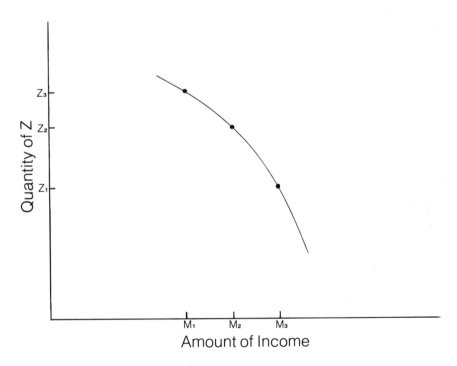

FIG. 2.12.   AN ENGEL CURVE FOR AN INFERIOR GOOD

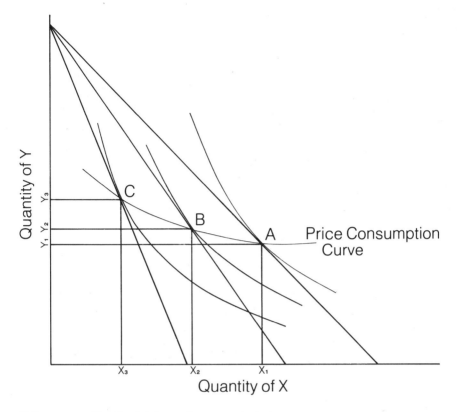

FIG. 2.13.   EFFECT OF CHANGE IN PRICES ON CHOICE

to that shown in the next budget line, consumption (point B) is
X_2 of X and Y_2 of Y. The person in this case substitutes Y for X
because of the X price increase. If the price of X increased still
further, so the inward-most budget line applies, the choice
becomes X_3 and Y_3 (at point C). The curve which connects all of
these choices under the varying price ratios is the price-consumption curve.

   The price-consumption curve need not slope downward as in
Fig. 2.13. An upward sloping price-consumption curve may
occur (Fig. 2.14). Here, an increase in the price of X also results
in less X consumed, but not as much less as in Fig. 2.13. The
remaining cutback in consumption made necessary by the price
increase of X is taken through good Y. In this case, the consumer
acquired less of both goods. An increase in the price of X may
also leave the consumption of Y unaffected (Fig. 2.15). All of the

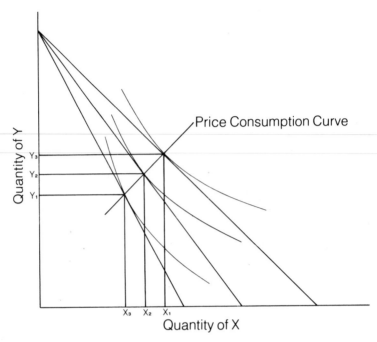

FIG. 2.14.   EFFECT OF PRICE INCREASE OF X ON BOTH Y AND X

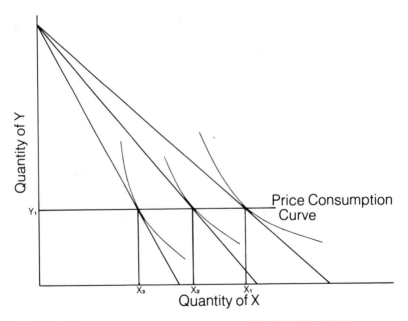

FIG. 2.15.   EFFECT OF PRICE INCREASE OF X ON RELATIVE
AMOUNTS OF X AND Y PURCHASED

effect is absorbed by X. The consumer still spends the same amount of money on X as before. With a fixed money income M, fixed price of Y and (as shown) quantity of Y, the amount spent on Y is constant so the amount spent on X must be constant. The quantity of X consumed decreases in direct proportion to the price (of X) increase. This price-consumption curve is horizontal.

The consumer could also have a vertical price-consumption curve (Fig. 2.16). Here, even though the price of X may change, the consumer must have a given amount of X and only that amount. This involves strong preferences for the commodity or service. Some medicines could fit in this category.

From the information presented in the price-consumption curve, one can construct a demand curve. The demand curve relates the prices of a good to the quantity of the good consumed at each price. The consumer knows the prices of X and uses them in constructing the budget lines. One can then read from the

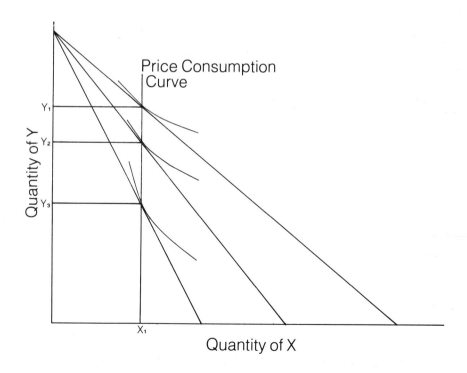

FIG. 2.16.   EFFECT OF PRICE INCREASE OF X ON QUANTITY OF Y PURCHASED RELATIVE TO X

graph the X_1, X_2 and X_3, which correspond to each price and relate them directly to the prices (Fig. 2.17). The X axis is the same as in Fig. 2.13 and the prices were implicit in the budget lines. The demand curve, unlike the price-consumption curve, always slopes downward. The Law of Demand states that the price and quantity demanded of a good are inversely related, if other factors are held constant.

While the demand curve always slopes downward, its slope may vary. This brings us to a new question. Given that quantity demanded will decrease as price increases, by how much will it decrease with respect to a given price increase? The previous price-consumption curves indicate considerable variation. A

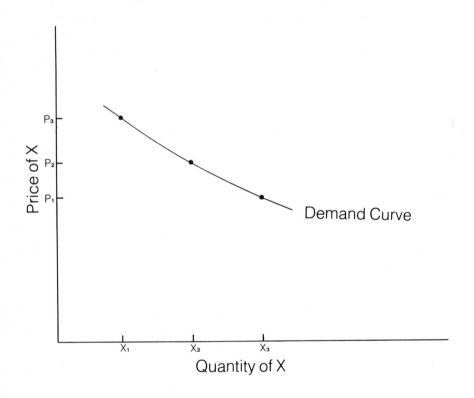

FIG. 2.17.   A   RELATIVELY ELASTIC DEMAND CURVE

large decline in X consumption is shown in Fig. 2.13, less is shown in Fig. 2.15, still less in Fig. 2.14 and none in Fig. 2.16. The demand curves, derived from the information in price-consumption curves, should reflect this variation. Fig. 2.18 corresponds to Fig. 2.14, Fig 2.19 to Fig. 2.15, Fig. 2.20 to Fig. 2.16.

Elasticity

The concept of elasticity describes *by how much*. Price elasticity is defined as the percentage change in quantity demanded per percentage change in price. If one compares two points on

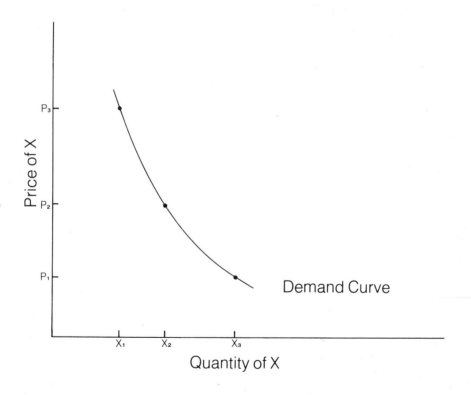

FIG. 2.18.   A   RELATIVELY INELASTIC DEMAND CURVE

the demand curve, an approximation to price elasticity would be the formula:

$$E = -\frac{\dfrac{Q_2 - Q_1}{(Q_2 + Q_1)/2}}{\dfrac{P_2 - P_1}{(P_2 + P_1)/2}}$$

Where X absorbs a greater than proportional share of the effect, E will exceed 1 (Fig. 2.17 and 2.13). Here, X is termed a relatively elastic good. Where all the effect is taken by X, $E=1$, i.e., the percentage change in quantity demanded exactly equals the percentage change in price (Fig. 2.19 and 2.15). This is called unit elasticity. In Fig. 2.18 and 2.14, although some decrease in X consumption occurs, it does not suffice for adjustment to the new circumstances; Y consumption also decreases. Therefore, X shows a decline less than proportionate to the price change, $E<1$ and X becomes a relatively inelastic good. In Fig. 2.16 and 2.20, X shows no change; the numerator of the equation is zero, so $E=0$ and X is perfectly inelastic.

Elasticity of quantity demanded with respect to income works in the same way as price elasticity. The two-point formula becomes:

$$E = \frac{\dfrac{Q_2 - Q_1}{(Q_2 + Q_1)/2}}{\dfrac{M_2 - M_1}{(M_2 + M_1)/2}}$$

For a good whose consumption strongly responds to changes in income, known as a superior or an income elastic good, the $E>1$; for a normal or an income inelastic good the $E<1$ but also $E>0$; for an inferior good, the $E<0$.

As mentioned, the income elasticity of a good largely reflects the luxury, the necessity and the affordable quality aspects of the good. Price elasticity also has its major determinants. The primary determinant is the number and closeness of available substitutes for the good. For example, consider the soft drink

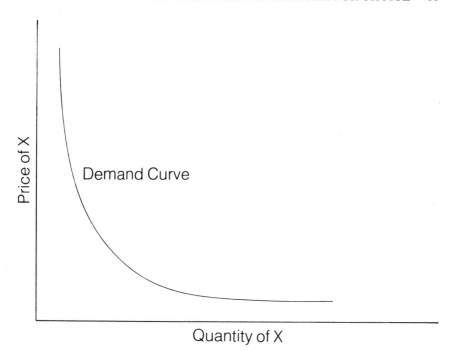

FIG. 2.19.   A DEMAND CURVE WITH UNIT ELASTICITY

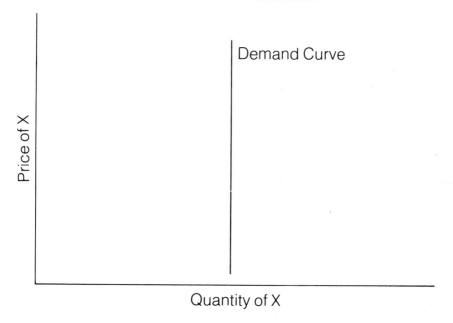

FIG. 2.20.   A PERFECTLY INELASTIC DEMAND CURVE

market in which there exist many similar products which satisfy the same need. If Coca-Cola raised its price while Pepsi and Royal Crown and the other colas did not, many Coke drinkers would undoubtedly switch to a cheaper cola. One would expect the price elasticity of Coca-Cola to be relatively high. On the other hand, coffee has fewer close substitutes; tea probably forms the only close one. A rise in coffee prices as happened in 1977 did not significantly decrease coffee consumption; the price elasticity of coffee is very low.

Another factor involved in price elasticity is the expensiveness of a good relative to the consumer's total budget. If the price of a candy bar increases by 25%, this does not have nearly the impact that a 25% increase in car prices will. An extra nickel probably will not cause great sacrifices for the candy buying consumer, therefore the price elasticity of candy will be low, but an extra $1000 just might cause sacrifices for the car buyer so the price elasticity of the car should be higher.

A third factor becomes the time horizon in which elasticity is considered. A consumer who has time to adjust to a price increase by developing new preferences or finding new substitutes will more likely do so and decrease consumption of the original product than a consumer confronted with an immediate need which must be fulfilled. The former case will be more price elastic than the latter.

Effects of Related Goods

The above analysis of quantity desired of a good with respect to its price considers the effects of preferences through the use of indifference curves and the price of that good itself. It assumes that prices of other related goods are constant. If prices of other goods do change, they affect the demand curve for the original good depending on the kind of relationship that exists between them.

Substitute goods fulfill the same needs as seen in the soft drink market. If the price of Coke went up, the quantity consumed of Coke would decrease and the quantity consumed of Pepsi or other soft drinks would rise to compensate for it (Fig. 2.21). At the same Pepsi price, more Pepsi would be demanded (Q^1) than before (Q). This shifts the demand curve to the right or outward.

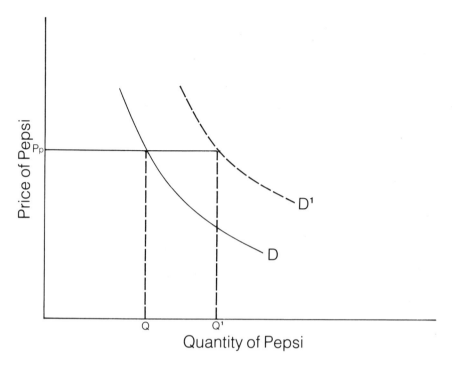

FIG. 2.21.   A SHIFT IN DEMAND CURVE FOR PEPSI AS RESULT OF
INCREASE IN PRICE FOR COKE (GOOD SUBSTITUTES)

A decrease in the price of Coke would have the reverse effect;
Pepsi drinkers would switch to the cheaper substitute.

   Complementary goods tend to be used together. If the price of
steak increases, the quantity of steak consumed goes down and
the quantity of steak sauce used also goes down. In the steak
sauce market, for a given price of steak sauce less now is consumed (Q^1) than before (Q), because of the rise in price of the
complementary steak which shifted the steak sauce demand
curve inward (Fig. 2.22). The reverse would happen for a decrease in steak prices.

   The basic framework for economic analysis then involves the
operation of consumer preferences (the indifference curve) on
the range of possibilities the consumer faces. The two major
forces then become preferences and constraints on those preferences. This framework with the assumed motivation of utility
maximization will be considered in various contexts throughout
the following pages.

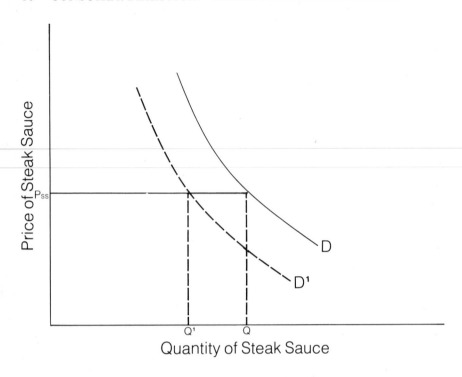

FIG. 2.22.   A SHIFT IN DEMAND CURVE FOR STEAK SAUCE AS RESULT OF INCREASE IN PRICE OF STEAK (GOOD COMPLEMENTS)

APPLICATION OF THEORIES

The Price Elasticity of Shampoo
by Grace A. Shieh

The price elasticity of demand refers to the amount by which people increase or decrease their purchases when the price changes. Whenever the percentage change in quantity demanded is *greater* than the percentage change in price of the product(s)—demand is said to be elastic. Whenever the percentage change in quantity demanded is *less* than the percentage change in price of the product(s)—demand is said to be inelastic. This elasticity or responsiveness depends upon the importance of the price relative to one's income, but even moreso upon the quality and price of available substitutes.

Looking at shelves of shampoo at the store makes it obvious that a consumer can choose among many different brands and types, each brand and type of shampoo being a substitute for a different one. However, the product itself, set apart in its own category, has no substitute.

In general people today are not likely to wash their hair with soap or home-made preparations. Soaps have been known to deposit scum on the hair shafts, thus, reducing sheen. Home-made preparations require ingredients which take time to obtain and properly combine. With the advent of synthetic detergents in shampoo, desirable properties in them have left little room for shampoo substitutes. Due to its nature, it is generally agreed that each brand and type of shampoo is a relatively elastic good. Specifically and by itself, shampoo in its own category is considered to be a relatively inelastic good. This implies that a similar quantity of the good will be demanded regardless of minor price fluctuations. However, with more good substitutes for a particular shampoo than for all shampoos, we have moved from a very inelastic to what is probably a highly elastic demand for the same quantity. That is the reason why people are not victimized when they purchase shampoo. They might be willing to pay three dollars a bottle if shampoo was not available at a lower price. Fortunately, though, there are many options. A seller who tried to take advantage of the fact that the total demand for shampoo is relatively inelastic would lose his/her customers, the demand for *the shampoo he/she sells* will be quite elastic.

The Growth of Consumer Credit
by David Sills

Credit has been present in American society since Colonial times. Credit policies used then were known as "open book credit." This credit was extended to merchants who owned the stores. There was no formal contract involved with this type of credit. Because of the basic insecurity of the credit arrangement, merchants generally only extended credit to the more prominent members of society. In return for the goods the consumer would promise to pay the merchant either when he was paid, if he was a wage earner, or when his crops were harvested, if he was a farmer. In this way, open book credit took the form of short-term credit in the case of the wage earner who was paid weekly or monthly. It also provided longer-term credit for the farmer who received his pay annually when he harvested his crops. This situation came about usually out of necessity rather than choice. If the merchant did not extend credit it was unlikely that he could achieve enough cash sales to operate his business (Natl. Retail Merchants' Assoc. 1969).

The second development in consumer credit (installment-credit) was more applicable to durables. The merchandise acquired on credit was also the collateral. Usually a down payment was required and a contract was drawn up with payments to be made over specified increments of time. This provided the merchant with more security and enabled him to extend credit to a larger segment of the population. It is believed that cash customers were given a discount. This meant that credit customers were paying an interest charge for use of the money necessary to acquire the merchant's goods. Credit policies did not change much from the early 1800s until just after World War II. The great Depression caused a temporary dip in the quantity of credit offered as did the introduction of legislation restricting the extension of credit.

The credit card as we know it today was first introduced on a large-scale basis by airlines and railroads in 1947 and by Diners Club in 1949. Generally there is a 30-day period where the user may pay his bill without any interest being assessed on his account. Any balance remaining after this period is subject to an annual interest charge of between 12% and 18%. Initially, these cards were used as a convenience to pay for travel and entertainment expenses. This necessarily restricted their use to wealthier people (Anon. 1969).

From 1945 until the present the use of credit by Americans has been increasing at a remarkable rate. This fact is borne out by the 1968 Economic Report to the President (see Table 2.1).

In this section, an economic analysis of the effect credit has upon a consumer is presented. For simplicity, a consumer's choice of consumption of a single product (C) is considered. Consumption of this product is considered over two separate time periods (C_0 and C_1). The horizontal axis of the graph repre-

TABLE 2.1.   NET DEBT AND GROSS NATIONAL PRODUCT (in billions of dollars)

Year	Total	Federal	State	Corpo- rate	Farm	Mort- gage	Commercial and Financial	Cons- umer	GNP
1935	180	38	16	76	9	24	11	6	83
1946	397	230	14	94	8	33	12	8	209
1956	708	225	43	232	20	121	24	43	419
1966	1345	279	101	497	42	279	52	95	743

Source: Anon. (1967).

sents present consumption (C_0) and the vertical axis represents consumption in the following period (C_1). The optimum position will depend upon the individual's preferences and opportunities (see Fig. 2.23).

The problems an individual faces with an intertemporal decision are in principle no different from the corresponding problems of consumption of X and Y within a single time period (Fig. 2.24). An individual will have a unique indifference map (indifference curves U_1, U_2, U_3) and a consumption opportunity set

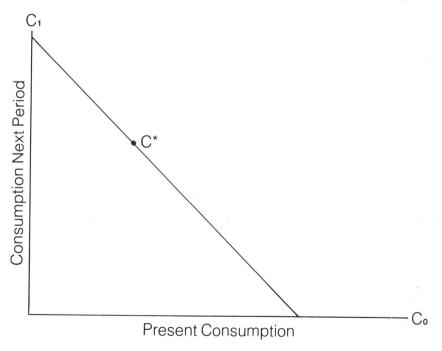

FIGURE 2.23.

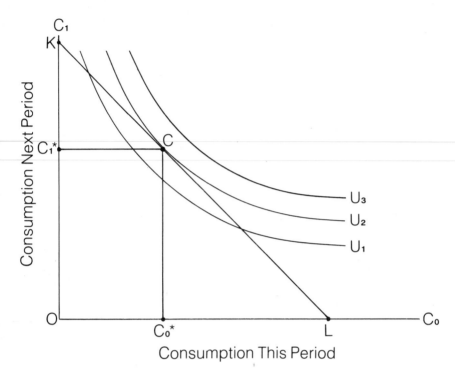

FIGURE 2.24.

(K, L). The optimum for the consumer will be the point of tangency (C*). This represents the "consumption basket" that takes the form of an intertemporal stream of consumption where C_0* represents current consumption and C_1* represents future consumption.

At this point, special terminology must be employed for the analysis of the consumer's intertemporal choice. Note that the budget line (K, L) goes through an intertemporal endowment position at C*. This is the position where the consumer is neither borrowing nor lending, which would take the form of saving. He consumes C_0* this period and anticipates C_1* next period. His indifference map would shift down and to the right as shown in Fig. 2.25 if the individual were to provide increased consumption in the current period given market and personal financial conditions. This would mean an increase in C_0* and a decrease in C_1*. The consumer could accomplish this by use of a credit card or borrowing from an institution.

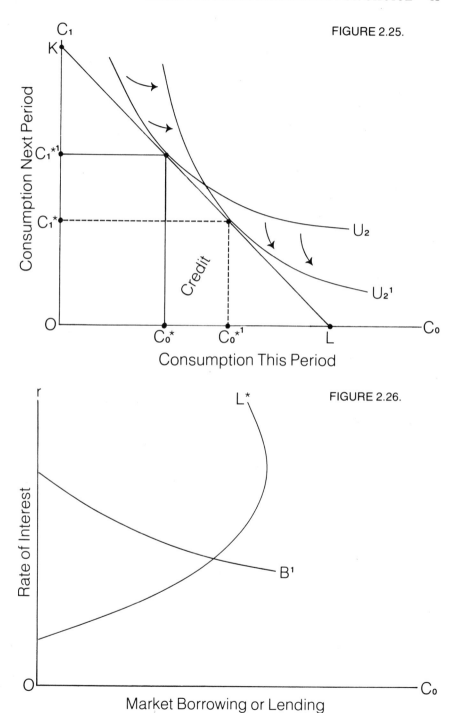

FIGURE 2.25.

FIGURE 2.26.

Factors such as the interest rate on credit and the endowed wealth of the individual are constraints upon the quantity of product C which can be consumed. Thus, these two factors determine the budget line (K, L). By imagining different prices (interest rates) and different quantities of wealth possessed by the individual a price expansion path may be constructed (Fig. 2.26). These curves can be translated into supply and demand curves for the individual and the market as a whole. From these supply and demand curves an equilibrium rate of interest may be found where the supply and demand for credit will be equal (Hirshleifer 1976).

REFERENCES

ANON. 1967. Consumer credit in family financial management. *In* Proc. of Natl. Workshop. Amer. Home Econ. Assoc., Washington, D.C.

HIRSHLEIFER, J. 1976. Price Theory and Applications. Prentice-Hall, New Jersey.

NATL. RETAIL MERCHANTS' ASSOC. 1969. Economic Characteristics of Department Store Credit. International Copyright Union, New York.

3

Broadening the Economic Concepts

So far, the basics of conventional economic analysis have been described. However, the tools of economic analysis need not remain in the traditional setting of two physical goods and no good reason exists not to include deeper analysis of some of the ceteris paribus assumptions, such as the formation of preferences.

Some previous efforts have been made. Katona (1951) for example, has pleaded for years for greater interaction between economics and psychology and has indicated some of the ways in which this interaction could be beneficial. Lancaster (1966) has broadened the meaning of the labels on the axes to include characteristics of the goods rather than the physical goods themselves as the items between which the consumer chooses. Becker (1976) supports the application of economic theory to many nonmonetary situations. These steps, while in the right direction, do not go nearly as far as the matter could be taken. For example, Becker does not attempt to integrate the research done in other social sciences into economic analysis. These other fields explore areas which economists traditionally have assumed constant, such as preferences, or relegated conventional definitions, i.e., prices. With proper definitions of terms, economics and the other social sciences, particularly psychology, could become truly complementary disciplines. The economic framework can analyze a variety of noneconomic phenomena, and the psychological theories and research can give greater precision to economic theory.

To begin with, the labels on the axes refer to alternatives in this particular situation. The basic budget line/indifference curve analysis represents only one decision at one point in time and in one context. This is usually not explicitly stated but should be implicit in the analysis. Thus, the decision depends on the situation and no reason exists to assume that "a rose is a rose is a rose," or that a bathing suit on the beach carries the same connotations as a bathing suit in a store or a bathing suit on the street. Evaluation of alternatives may vary with the situation, which obviously affects the indifference curve map and perhaps the perceived budget line as well by including social disapproval as part of the cost of choosing the bathing suit.

One also need not limit the elements on the axes to specific, tangible goods. The choice may be between intangible activities, for example, between time spent studying for a course and time spent playing ball. Lancaster chose to state the tradeoff as between characteristics of the goods involved. The choice could also be between intangible qualities, which then would imply behavior to reach them. For example, a person may face a tradeoff between social conformity and individuality. One may be obtained only at the expense of the other. The person will have a set of preferences and the particular society may decide the price, such as how much individuality it will allow before it defines the behavior as a deviation from the norm. The person will likely choose a mixture of the two, conforming to some degree or in some aspects, but not totally. In this example, behavior is implied by the choice rather than defined by the choice.

It should be obvious by now that as the axes need not be defined in the traditional way, neither must the budget line be defined conventionally or in objective monetary terms. The budget line reflects "reality," or the limitations the person faces in the situation as perceived by the person. Again, this is heavily individualistic. The person will only act on the basis of such information as he/she possesses which may not be the information given to someone else and that information, even in the identical situation, may vary widely with the person. People do not perceive experiences identically. Therefore, in considering the nature of the budget line, one should begin by considering perception and other cognitive activities.

BUDGET LINE: THE PERSON'S "REALITY"

Perception: Acquisition of Information

Obviously, an individual will react only to experiences he/she perceives and this reaction will depend on the way in which that experience is perceived. No two people will have the identical perception of an experience because people are not identical. The way a person is "set" to perceive the world depends on past experience, and reflects the individual's physiological and psychological characteristics as well as the person's social environment. A person's perception of an experience is referred to occasionally as the mental impression that person has of the experience.

The major determinants of perception can be classified as structural and functional. The structural factors refer to the nature of the physical stimulus, that is, the actual experience. For example, a person's physiological system most likely will not perceive a chair as a table. The philosophical question will be waived concerning whether such a thing as concrete experience really exists or whether it is all in the mind of the individual.

The functional factors refer to factors within the individual, for example, psychological factors. Bruner and Goodman (1947) studied the effect of need on perception. From their findings that poor children perceived coins to be larger than did rich children, two hypotheses were formed as general laws as follows.

(1) The greater the social value of an object, the more will it be susceptible to organization by behavioral determinants.
(2) The greater the individual need for a socially valued object, the more marked will be the operation of behavioral determinants.

Since money has a high social value, and the poor children had a greater need for it, the perception by poor children of money was more likely to be influenced by factors other than the physical characteristics of the coins.

Other functional factors may also operate. Asch (1951) found that among subjects who conformed to the incorrect opinion of the majority, several actually had thought that the majority was correct. They conformed but were not aware of doing so since they had unconsciously adopted the majority's "perception" as their own.

In this case, social factors had a strong influence. Two basic propositions concerning perception will be considered.

(1) People will impose some organization on their perceptions and will ascribe some meaning to them. A classic example illustrating this tendency concerns the American school child listening to foreign language Christmas carols. When invited to sing along with "O Tannenbaum," the child sang "Atomic Bomb, Atomic Bomb." The child knew no German; "Atomic Bomb" was his best attempt to make sense out of what he was singing. Another example of organizing and ascribing meaning to physical stimuli is the familiar pastime of identifying constellations in the sky. Instead of contentedly perceiving a random array of stars, we identify the Big Dipper, Little Dipper, Cassandra, Gemini and many more.

A person doesn't wait for all the information concerning an experience to come in before forming an impression of it. As soon as the person receives any information, he/she forms an impression and will organize future information into the meaningful whole implied by the first. First impressions of personality are important because the first impression is organized. This organization establishes the expected pattern and further information details the initial organization. This also may account for reluctance to abandon a theory even in the face of contrary evidence, at least until a clearly superior theory (organization) appears as an alternative. The organization may also infer other information which was not presented. For example, if a person perceives politicians to be shrewd and has the information "politician," he/she may perceive the quality of shrewdness as well.

(2) Perception is functionally selective. No one perceives everything that is "out there" to be perceived. For example, a spectator at a football game has a wide range of perceptual possibilities: the game itself, the action on the field and within that action is the movement of the ball, the quarterback's actions, and the backfield. There is also the action in the stands,

for example, the vendor hawking hotdogs, the opposing team's cheering section, the cheerleaders, the rowdy fraternity seated above with their smuggled half-pint flasks or the couple seated below providing their own R-rated show. The weather also may claim the person's attention especially if it is cold or rainy. But each spectator will not be aware of everything in the stadium at once. Some experiences will claim dominance in the person's general perception of the game. For the football fanatic, it may be the action on the field. For the person who is there on a date without having any knowledge of football, it may be the action in the stands. For a Women's Christian Temperance Union member, it may be the rowdy fraternity. Obviously, each person's selection of items from the perceptual field differs. The general hypothesis concerning selective perception is that "The objects that play the major role in the organized perception, the objects that are accentuated, are usually those objects which serve some immediate purpose of the perceiving individual" (Krech and Crutchfield 1948).

A classic example of this appeared in an investigation of a Dartmouth-Princeton football game (Hastorf and Cantril 1954). Supporters of each team, when shown the same game film, perceived items favorable to their team. For example, Princeton supporters saw the Dartmouth team make more violations of the rules than the Dartmouth supporters saw Dartmouth make. "In brief, the data here indicate that there is no such "thing" as a "game" existing "out there" in its own right which people merely "observe." The "game" exists for a person and is experienced by him only in so far as certain happenings have significances in terms of his purpose. Out of all the occurrences going on in the environment, a person selects those that have some significance for him from his own egocentric position in the total matrix... From this point of view, it is inaccurate and misleading to say that different people have different "attitudes" concerning the same "thing." For the "thing" simply is *not* the same for different people whether the "thing" is a football game, a presidential candidate, Communism or spinach" (Hastorf and Cantril 1954).

Obviously there are many factors which affect perceptual selectivity. The needs of the perceiving individual influence what the individual perceives. The Princeton supporter perceived a game more favorable to Princeton; the Dartmouth supporter had perceptions which favored Dartmouth. As mentioned previously in the case of poor children and rich children in their perceptions of coins, the poor children's needs differed from those of the rich children.

The person's mental set will also be important. A person may be primed to expect to perceive in a certain way. If so, he/she is likely to in fact perceive the expected pattern. A policeman on the alert for a criminal activity is more likely to perceive it than the average unsuspecting citizen. Given the same deteriorating community, a policeman, social worker and resident will likely perceive it in different ways simply because they are *set* to perceive different facets of the community.

The person may also perceive differently according to his/her mood. The happy person may "look at the world through rose-colored glasses," and as such sees a different picture than does the person who is generally depressed. One group of experimenters (Leuba and Lucas 1945) induced different moods in the same subjects by hypnosis and noted the difference in the subject's descriptions of the same picture. They found considerable difference in these perceptions according to whether the subject was in the happy, critical or anxious mood.

Culture also affects perception. The norms of the culture or society in which the person has been brought up and the beliefs the person has all affect what the person will perceive in a situation. In the football game situation, the WCTU member would be especially sensitive to the presence of alcohol in the stands. An Oriental pacifist philosopher may "perceive" the senseless violence on the field. The football fan may see a healthy, physical exercise and the skill of the players.

Given, at least, that one does not consciously perceive everything to be perceived, the next question becomes *why*. Some factors affecting selective perception have been identified, but how do these operate? Intuition may answer that a person just does not pay attention to everything which goes on. In other words, a process of selective attention operates. What one attends to may depend on needs, moods, mental set, etc., at a particular time.

Considerable disagreement exists among the psychological researchers as to how precisely attention operates or even whether attention is a necessary concept. Neisser (1976), for example, holds that attention is nothing but perception. An individual chooses what will be seen by anticipating the structured information it will provide. One chooses what will be heard by actively engaging him or herself with it, not by shutting out its competitors. Therefore, attention models which impose a selective filter on the world of experience are unnecessary. Neisser criticizes attention theorists for treating the mind as a passive, fixed mechanism and ignoring the free choice or the voluntary control by the person. He claims that much of the individual's perceptual capacity is flexible, due to the efforts and skills of the person.

Neisser relies heavily on perceptual schemata (frameworks, sets of expectations concerning the environment) for which attention is unnecessary to guide the person's cognitive activity. These do not require processing of information since the information is already in the stimulus perceived. More information simply results in a more specified schema with which the person anticipates new information. Neisser speaks of a "perceptual cycle" by which experience and perception continually interact and modify each other. Past experience contributing to a person's mental set influences perception, as previouly indicated. However, although one cannot perceive unless he/she anticipates, he/she need not see only what is anticipated. An individual's set of expectations may be modified by new experiences. It is these expectations rather than attention which guide what is perceived.

The perceptual cycle is illustrated by a diagram (Fig. 3.1). People have certain expectations concerning the environment, including a schema of the present environment. These expectations direct their activity as they act in accordance with what they *know* about the world, including perceptual activity. This activity will be a sample of the actual environment and obtained by coming into contact with it. The sample will not be a 100% sample. The information picked up from the environment through this activity will then modify the set of expectations to the extent that the experience is not totally consistent with previous expectations. This revised schema then continues the cycle. For example, if a persons' mental image of a dog is an animal like a great dane, the information that a poodle is also a dog will require a modification of what a person expects when he/she

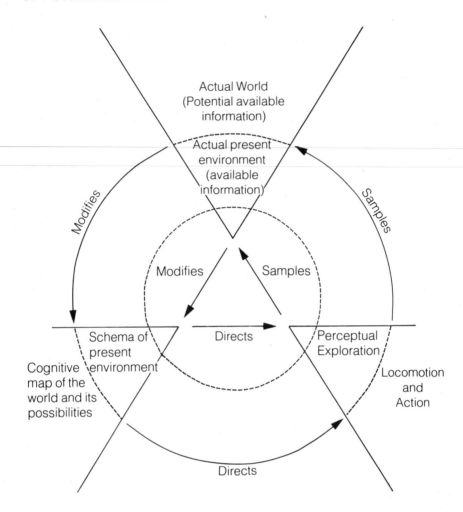

FIG. 3.1.   A PERCEPTUAL CYCLE

sees a dog. Nowhere in Neisser's model does attention operate.

Those researchers who feel the need for a theory of attention disagree as to whether people actually selectively perceive or whether they in fact perceive everything but simply do not (or cannot) process it all. Broadbent (1958) and Triesman (1964) hold that people selectively perceive, and this selective perception is governed by attention. A person must process the information in the environment. As a person does not have unlimited capacity for processing information, a selective filter operates between all the sensory experiences and the processing channel. In other words, attention determines what goes through the processes of perception, and the person concentrates on one channel of information at a time. The processing of the information constitutes the perception of the information, and attention determines what gets processed and therefore perceived. This model does not easily explain how a person's attention may momentarily shift to something else. To that extent, Broadbent and Triesman also require some voluntary control by the person, in that the person may choose to "set" him/herself to be receptive to a particular channel.

Deutsch and Deutsch (1963) on the other hand focus on the person's selection of the response he/she will make rather than on the selection of stimuli to which he/she will attend. By this view, the person processes every sensory experience but attention operates at the level of memory and action rather than at perception. The person perceives everything, but does not retain everything in his/her memory so he/she may not be aware later of having perceived some items. Which events the person retains depends on their pertinence; the person makes a choice of which events to retain. Deutsch and Deutsch make a sharp distinction between perception and memory, a distinction which involves attention. Broadbent and Triesman make the distinction between sensory store (very temporary store of sensory experience) and the perceptual process. When the person is at any later time aware of having perceived something, a chain of processing thus develops from sensory store to perception to memory. For Broadbent and Triesman, attention governs what is perceived; for Deutsch and Deutsch, attention governs what is remembered.

Kahneman (1973) holds that a person's cognitive system has limited processing resources available; therefore, the person must allocate these resources in some way. Here, attention and effort both play a role. The items to which a person will give his/her attention, and therefore allocate his/her processing resources, are determined by a series of such factors as:

(1) "enduring dispositions," which refer to factors influencing involuntary attention;

(2) monetary intentions, which refer in the experimental setting to the instructions given the subject by the experimenter;

(3) evaluation of demands (with two or more allocation possibilities) which involves deciding which is more worth attending to; and

(4) effects of arousal, with higher levels of arousal increasing performance to a certain point after which performance decreases.

With higher levels of arousal the person's capacity expands somewhat. This concurs with Neisser's proposal of flexibility of a person's perceptual capacity. This model is extremely general and hard to evaluate, but it does indicate some of the major factors involved.

Memory: The Information Store

After the person has selectively perceived the environment, how does this perception become translated and retained as information for the person's future decisions?

Early psychological research limited its focus to the acquisition of information and the long-term retention of that information. In more recent years, theories based on a more or less linear processing model have considered at least two different forms of memory process—that for immediate events and that for permanent storage of information. A person's memory depends on the presentation of the material and the attention given to this material. The person can attend to only that which is available to be perceived. The person can remember only that which he/she has attended to and perceived, depending somewhat on which attention model one uses.

The process again begins with the limited-capacity sensory store, the temporary (almost fleeting) store of sensory experience. There exist both visual and auditory stores corresponding to the person's encounter of the experience through his/her eyes or ears. The person usually cannot encode for further processing all the experience present in this sensory store and as such may lose some of it. The experience in the store may be displaced by new experiences. Any experience not displaced may rapidly decay from the store. Loss of experience appears to happen primarily because of the interference from other experiences, rather than from a decay of the experience in itself. To retain the information from the experience, the person must process it into short term memory. The person uses some categorization process in order to do this, some process of contact between the sensory input and the more stable long term memory. In this categorization process a label from long term memory is attached to the image in the sensory store.

One way to retain information in short term memory is by constant repetition (rehearsal). For example, to retain a telephone number long enough to dial it, a person may repeat it over and over en route to the phone and while dialing. The categorization process consists of retrieving from long term memory the words or numerals associated with the sounds of the operator's voice or with the configuration of black dots on the directory page. Some preliminary coding of material in the sensory store takes place before this contact with long term memory takes place; that is, some organized image forms in the sensory store which then becomes labeled. Short term memory also has limited capacity and duration. Its information is not particularly organized, so one must search the entire (short term) memory to retrieve a certain bit of information.

Long term memory on the other hand is a permanent storage system of unlimited capacity. Its meaningful organization, at least meaningful to the person, enables the person to retrieve information. Researchers disagree over the precise form of this organization, but a hierarchical system of categories appears to exist. For example, to remember a detail of Freudian theory, one might first think of the introductory psychology course one had, then of the subset of that course dealing with personality, then of the major theorists covered in that section, then of Freud. As such, one needs to retain far fewer bits of information simultanously than if one tried to remember the entire course content of one's university career without this organization. Researchers have found that if one is presented with a series of

items, one best recalls the first items, hypothetically because
these have received the most processing into long term memory,
and the last items because these are still in short term memory.
"Forgetting" material from long term memory generally results
from simply losing the organizational keys; the material still
exists in long term memory but is no longer accessible. Mne-
monic devices facilitate retrieval from long term memory. For
example, a rhyme like "30 days have September, April, June and
November" provides an additional organization to the material,
assuming one remembers the organization pattern.

The processing seems to take place in a more or less linear
fashion. However, some evidence indicates that material may
flow in the opposite direction; once it has arrived in long term
memory, it may be retrieved from there. Still, these stages
represent different aspects of the memory process. The person
first experiences and registers material in the sensory store,
then processes that material which has not already decayed from
the store into short-term memory. The person then further
processes much, although not all, of this material in short term
memory and organizes it into long term memory. He/she then
refers to this long term memory for his/her prior information
concerning a particular subject.

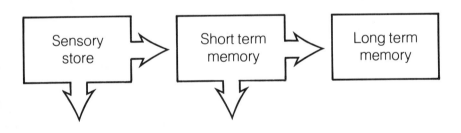

FIG. 3.2.   STAGES OF MEMORY PROCESS

As previously indicated, the budget line represents reality as
perceived by the person and this "reality" may vary greatly
among individuals. Wide individual variation exists in perception of the same situation and one should not expect retention of
the same material to be identical among individuals either. In

the individual's consideration of the limitations he/she faces in a given situation, he/she will rely not only on immediate experience but also on past experience and otherwise acquired information concerning this type of situation.

Perceived Price and Income

Although in economic theory the budget line refers to price and income, these concepts need not be taken solely in the monetary sense. For example, the person always faces some sort of price in any situation because any action involves some cost: if nothing else, the opportunity cost due to the time required to perform it. A person who reads this page gives up the time which he/she could spend playing ball or reading a novel. The perceived cost to the person will most likely vary with the person. For example, an individual contemplating use of illegal drugs faces not only the monetary cost of purchasing the drugs, but also the risk of discovery, arrest and subsequent penalties, and legal or family pressure. The latter risks form an element of the total price of the illegal drug; if the drug is legalized, the total perceived price should drop due to the risk element. If the person does not know the drug is illegal, the perceived price on the basis of which he/she will act will be far less than perhaps objectively it should be. The difference in experience forms another basis for difference in perceived price across individuals. One individual may see little risk involved; perhaps he/she stands to lose little if caught. Another individual may fear he/she may jeopardize his/her job, friends and/or family relationships if discovered. The latter individual faces a much higher perceived price than does the former. Perceived risk, therefore, affects perceived price by introducing an added element to the cost. In terms of risky decision-making, this adds another incentive for the person to minimize the risk involved.

The price a person faces may not even contain any monetary element at all. Social norms involve a relative cost between two alternatives. A socially defined immoral activity carries a relatively high price for the person contemplating it. There is even a maximum quantity restriction similar to the economic budget line in that if the person performs enough immoral activity he/she is put in jail where he/she cannot perform any more. A person who wishes to be a nonconformist must pay the sometimes quite high social price of nonacceptance or isolation, which is far less for a person who does not stand out from the crowd. A person who is highly dependent on social activity would perceive a much higher cost to isolation than would a "loner."

Price, then, means much more than simply monetary cost. It refers to social norms and constraints which the individual faces, time requirements for various activities, opportunity cost of choices, and risk involved for various alternatives. The constraints which the individual will consider will be based on the information which he/she possesses. All individuals do not necessarily have the same information due to exposure to different experiences and different perceptions of the same experience. The price an individual considers in making a choice is highly subjective.

Income may also be interpreted in terms more general than the purely monetary. One could define income as the total resources a person has available for use. This "income" may include but is not limited to monetary income.

Economic theory commonly translates wealth into equivalent income or services derived from wealth. Wealth is even more obviously analogous to total available resources. One only needs to expand the definition of "resources" to include psychological and sociological resources as well.

Many of the personality theorists postulate some sort of psychic energy in their systems as will be discussed later. This relatively fixed amount of psychic energy represents the total amount of energy the person has to devote to various psychological activities. This describes the psychological resources the person has.

All researchers seem to agree that the better adjusted the person, the more he/she can achieve. Therefore, one could possibly define resources as the psychological healthiness of the individual via whatever theory one wishes. Self-confidence could be included as an aspect of psychological health. Socially, one could consider as resources the extent of the person's base of social support, such as the extensiveness of a social network of friends and acquaintances and/or the degree of the person's acceptance by a relevant group. Again, theorists seem to agree that the broader the base for social support and the greater the social support, the better off the individual is. Aspiring politicians have long recognized this. Which, or how broad a definition of resources one uses depends, of course, on what is most relevant to the situation.

MOTIVATION

Motivation is very important to the study of behavior. Economic theory assumes that the person will seek to maximize his/her total utility or satisfaction in any given situation. Note that the utility maximization is for the person making the decision, not for anyone else. This makes the entire decision process highly dependent upon the individual person, especially the information on which the person acts as discussed earlier and what would most satisfy this person's individual needs. The individual's perceptions and needs may not coincide with those of or those which appear to an outside observer.

The maximization also depends on what would most satisfy the individual at the time of the decision. A person at the time of decision acts on the basis of certain priorities which may or may not change a few moments later. For example, a person crossing a busy street has the choice of waiting for the traffic light or jaywalking. At the moment he/she darts across the street, time takes precedence over safety. As he/she reflects on that decision while recuperating from the hospital bed, safety becomes the more important element. A dieter may have a sudden craving for a candy bar. The decision to eat it may later appear irrational when considered in light of the long-term weight loss goals, but at the time of the decision that decision maximizes the person's utility. The whole question of irrationality then becomes moot when considered from this light.

The psychological literature does not dispute the basic premise of utility maximization. The main question becomes what constitutes a person's satisfaction? The motivation and personality theorists, in addressing this question, attempt to become much more specific concerning the very general premise of economists.

One of the best known general views of motivation is Maslow's hierarchy of needs. Maslow (1943) presents a hierarchy of five kinds of needs; the person must have more or less chronically satisfied each of the lower levels before he/she may concentrate on satisfying the next higher level.

The most basic needs are the physiological needs, such as hunger, thirst, cold, sex, fatigue. These needs are relatively independent of each other and of other motivations. For example, a person's thirst does not imply hunger. In many cases a localized physical basis for the need exists, for example, hunger, thirst and sex. However, fatigue and maternal responses, which also have been classed as physiological needs, are not felt primarily in a specific area of the body.

The independence of the physiological needs from the other needs is not complete. The physiological needs may serve as channels for other needs and may be themselves partially satisfied by other activities. For example, consider the hunger need. A person who feels hunger may hunger more for comfort or love than for proteins. This has been frequently encountered in the treatment of overweight patients. On the other hand, the hunger need can be partially satisfied by other activities, such as smoking cigarettes. Some correlation exists between cigarette smoking and weight loss.

If all needs are unsatisfied, the physiological needs take precedence for the person and all other needs are pushed into the background. The satisfaction of the physiological needs then constitutes the person's utility. Researchers have concluded this from studies dealing with extreme food deprivation; in these cases, all the subject's thoughts center on food. A more common example is a hungry pet or baby who does not want to be petted or played with until after feeding.

However, when these needs are largely, not necessarily completely, chronically fulfilled, other higher order needs emerge and become dominant for the person. The process of satisfaction and turning to other needs then repeats itself. It is frequently observed that human wants have no end. This creates what Maslow calls a "hierarchy of prepotency." This hierarchy implies that gratification has equal importance with deprivation, because gratification of a relatively physiological need frees the person from concern with that need and lets other more social needs emerge. As those needs are satisfied they become unimportant in the individual's considerations.

The next level in the hierarchy are the safety needs. One does not often observe safety needs in adults, although one does observe a preference for the familiar and known. Some speculate that the needs for safety motivate the tendency to have a religion or other organizing view of the world.

Children provide a more obvious illustration. Children show a preference for a predictable, orderly world. Parental quarreling or divorce or a death in the family may provoke great anxiety in a child. Social workers also note that a child may cling to his/her parents, even if totally unloved or rejected by them, because the parents still provide safety and protection.

Love needs constitute the next level. Assuming the previous needs are satisfied, the person will want warm relationships with other people. Much of psychotherapy and clinical research concentrates on the satisfaction of these needs.

The person will next need the esteem of others and esteem from him/herself. This includes a desire for reputation, respect from others, recognition and importance. A desire for strength, achievement, adequacy and independence relates to the person's self-esteem. Satisfaction of these needs results in self-confidence; the thwarting of these needs can yield an inferiority complex and further personality disorders. The Adler school of psychoanalysis stressed these needs, which Freud ignored.

If all of the above needs have been reasonably well fulfilled, the person will experience a desire for self-fulfillment; that is, a desire to become everything he/she has the ability to be. Maslow describes this as a need for self-actualization. The way the person chooses to do this will vary greatly with the person, since people have differing abilities. For this need to emerge clearly the person must be basically satisfied in other respects; we know little about this need because of a shortage of subjects.

Maslow, then, has presented one theory of motivation. However, the personality theorists also had their own views on motivation as a component of their theories. Considering the widely different orientations of the various theorists, much agreement surprisingly does exist. The personality theories will be discussed later, but the motivational aspects deserve mention here.

A very common approach views the person as a psychic energy system (Levy 1970). This system resembles that of physics. A given amount of energy exists which can be neither created nor destroyed and which moves from regions of greater concentration to regions of lesser concentration. However, the energy is psychic rather than physical. The psychic energy is the motivation.

One of the earliest psychologists to adopt this view was Freud. Since he saw humankind as a species, sharing the same biology, he reasoned that they should also share the same psychic system. Two major principles underly his system. The first is determinism. According to Freud (Pervin 1975), everything has a cause, although since many behaviors have multiple causes one cannot easily assign a single cause to a behavior. The second is unconscious motivation. Most of the time individuals are unaware of their motives for performing given behaviors.

The psychic energy originates in the id. The id represents the biological forces affecting the person and serves as the reservoir of the psychic energy. The energy is structured in the form of instincts or drives, the most prominent of which are sex and aggression. These constitute the psychological representations of the corresponding physical drives. The id, which aims to satisfy these instincts, operates on the "pleasure principle." The pleasure principle or straight hedonism does not involve consideration of rationality or the environment.

The ego represents the environmental forces. It provides the system's contact with reality and includes perceptual processes, logic and reason. It aims to find a realistic way of satisfying the impulses of the id. If an appropriate object is not available, the ego must defer the id's gratification. In the meantime, it resorts to the unconscious, reality-distorting defense mechanisms, mainly repression, to block the id's impulses and the anxiety felt as a result of this blockage.

The superego represents the moral or social forces, the conscience of the person. All three types of forces battle for the person's psychic energy. Conflict between any of the forces produces anxiety which drains away psychic energy to deal with the anxiety and reduce the tension. This explains why many neurotics are constantly tired; much of their psychic energy goes into reducing anxiety.

Murray (1938) also saw the person as an energy system. The person's needs account for the ways in which this energy is used. Some needs, such as dominance, are associated with a disposition to discharge energy; other needs, such as passivity, are associated with a disposition to conserve energy. Murray, similar to Maslow, separates a person's needs into physiological and psychogenic needs. For Murray, the most important manifestations of a person's needs become their effects on his/her behavior. The Edwards Personal Preference Test, widely used in clinical settings, resulted from Murray's theory. Koponen (1960), using Edwards' test, found a relationship between expressed needs, demographic variables and products purchased.

Cattell (1959), whose theory will be discussed in more detail later, shared this view of the person as an energy system, but came to this conclusion from an empirical basis. It is particularly significant when theorists with totally different orientations arrive at the same conclusions.

For Freud, the biological forces of the id had dominance and greatest importance. The psychic energy itself was biological in nature. He therefore used an essentially biological motivation. The later neoanalysts, while accepting the basics of Freud's system, gave more weight to the ego and higher order social needs. For example, Adler (1966) stressed the striving for superiority, Horney (1945) focused on the family and insecurities arising from there, and Fromm (1941) gave his attention to the search for satisfying human relationships.

The psychic energy system involves tension reduction in the relief of anxiety. The motive of tension reduction recurs throughout other types of theories as well. Cognitive dissonance theory, which will be discussed later, assumes the motive to reduce the dissonance (tension) felt in inconsistency. The learning theorists employ the idea even more directly. Dollard and Miller (1950) and Hull (1943) postulate a motivation of satisfying and thereby reducing the person's drive which presumably has created tension within the organism. This drive may be either innate (physiological) or learned (which tends to be psychosocial), which again concurs with Maslow's theory. The accomplishment of this drive reduction constitutes reinforcement, which gives the person satisfaction.

Agreement on systems of motivation is not total. Here, Rogers is a major exception. Rogers, with his motives of actualization and self-actualization, seems to fit most closely at the top of Maslow's hierarchy, but even here the two theories are not the same.

Under Rogers' (1959) theory, the basic motivation of the organism is actualization, the process of maintaining and enhancing the organism. Primary (physiological) drives would be considered a subpart of actualization, i.e., the part of maintaining the organism. One of the functions of actualization is differentiation, i.e., of one's own organism from the environment. As a result, a self-concept develops in the person's awareness and a self-actualization motive differentiates out of the actualization motive. Rogers defines self-actualization as the tendency to maintain and enhance one's self-concept. The self-concept thus being enhanced need not be favorable and self-actualization need not be beneficial to the organism; here lies the difference in implications between Rogers' self-actualization and Maslow's self-actualization. Rogers' personality theory will be discussed in more detail later.

APPLICATION OF THEORIES

The Perception of Shampoo
by Grace A. Shieh

In order to get consumers to differentiate among the 650-odd shampoos now flooding the market, shampoo merchants find it necessary to peddle dreams. For example, people readily fall prey to these claims:

"Use Herbal Essence and step into a garden of earthly delights. Where every bubble smells of mysterious green herbs and freshly picked wildflowers...

"Use Wella Balsam: Nothing else can make your hair so beautiful, so shiny, so easy to comb...

"Use Clairol Sunshine Harvest: It will leave your hair looking just the way nature intended: healthy, lusciously clean, and shining like the sun" (Anon. 1976).

Interestingly, these claims reflect different individuals' responses to a product stimulus, namely, shampoo. According to Robertson (1970), their perception of a specific brand or type of shampoo is based on four principles: (1) selective perception, (2) organized perception, (3) perception depending upon stimulus factors, and (4) perception depending upon personal factors. These principles help explain why no two people perceive a product exactly the same. Each person sees things differently within a perceptual field. This perception or mental impression of a stimulus object greatly affects a consumer's response to a product stimulus, such as shampoo. As a result, people purchase that brand or type of shampoo which they "perceive" as satisfying their wants or needs.

Three levels of response were proposed by Bauer and Greyser in their discussion on the perception and screening of advertisements: the opportunity for exposure, conscious awareness and reaction beyond awareness (Robertson 1970). Consumers are constantly engaged in a progressive filtering of the mass of advertising to which they are exposed. According to Robertson (1970), the average consumer is potentially exposed to 1500 ads daily. However, he/she actually perceives (is consciously aware of) only 77 ads each day, and only about 12 of these ads produce behavior.

Shampoo properties and their effects are probably familiar to every television viewer. It is hard to imagine watching any favorite TV show without also being exposed to numerous commercials for shampoos. These include:

"...at least one nymph loping in slow motion across grassy glades under a bouncing, billowing halo of feminine glory; street construction crews and pedestrians paralyzed as their mass masculinity is sideswiped by a silken-tressed sylph out on the avenue for her morning undulation; elevator passengers elevated and blind dates struck dumb by a radiant-maned creature close enough for comfort; acres of skin, scalp and smirks emerging from showers with secrets that refuse to keep; a gossamer-topped tot dreamily enduring the camera's gaze while her gossamer-topped look-alike mother hums to her of the magic bottle they share; or, a bit of good news for blondes, brunettes and redheads who weren't born that way" (Hopkins 1975).

In essence, when a consumer selectively perceives a particular shampoo he/she is making a compromise between what he/she is given to see, is "set" to see, wants to see, or even wants to avoid seeing.

The meaning attached to stimuli by a person is his/her perceptual organization. This involves a compromise between the individual's personal interpretation of stimuli and the stimuli that are present. "Furthermore, the more ambiguity in the stimulus field (such as, in an advertisement), the more the opportunity for personal factors to govern organization" (Robertson 1970). This principle of stimulus ambiguity is used by psychologists to gain insight into the individual's self-concept.

In a recent test by *Consumer Reports*, it was interesting to find that male and female panelists had very different preferences. Three main reasons suggested themselves as accounting for the difference in opinions about the shampoos. Far more women than men used such after-shampoo products as hair sprays, rinses or conditioners. Fifty percent of the women wore shoulder length hair; only 10% of the males did. And 38% of the women had tinted or dyed hair, compared to 3% of the men. Such differences indicate that male and female consumers require very different things of a shampoo.

Noting how shampoos are advertised, the fragrance preferences provide another explanation for the differing outlooks on shampoo. "Most shampoo advertising is aimed at women," says Robertson (1970), "the pitch often stresses pleasant fragrance and many shampoos today smell very sweet." Frequently, the dandruff-shampoo ads are aimed at men. These ads do not stress fragrance, presumably, because manufacturers feel a sweet fragrance would not be "manly" (Anon. 1976). Most dandruff shampoos have a medicinal smell.

About 95% of the panelists tested considered cleaning ability as a shampoo's most important characteristic. Their judgements of cleaning ability closely correlated with judgements of overall quality.

Contrast, intensity, frequency and movement are stimulus factors that determine perception. Commercials which have taken these factors into account have long been recognized by advertisers as key strategies in gaining message perception. Shampoo advertisements are very successful in accomplishing their purpose. They have even reached young children. One young 13-year-old from Glastonbury, Connecticut, comments: "When I see a beautiful girl using a shampoo on TV, I buy it because I'll look like her" (Waters 1977).

Personal factors which encourage perception include the individual's self-concept, needs, span of apprehension, mental set and past experiences. An individual who can identify with the person doing the shampoo advertisement is fulfilling his/her idea of self-concept. All the good qualities of the shampoo match his/her expectations of the product. Besides, he/she sees an image of him/herself in the model. The person's needs for a particular product, obviously, causes him/her to be more perceptive of the item. If an individual needs shampoo to wash his/her hair, he/she will filter out those messages pertaining to the different brands and types of shampoo. It is because this particular product is necessary in satisfying his/her needs. Although limiting perception, span of apprehension has been overcome by shampoo advertisers. A person can listen to the radio but cannot watch a television while driving a car; but, jingles and claims for different shampoos are just about everywhere: on the radio, on television, in magazines, on display stands and on billboards. The mental set, reflected in positive or negative moods, influences susceptibility to messages. If a person is feeling low, possibly trying a new and different shampoo will prove rewarding. Past experiences are perhaps the most important of all factors in a person's perception of a product. A shampoo not meeting the expectations of an individual will not most likely ever be purchased again by the same individual. If the claims of the advertisements have proven to be false, the consumer cannot be convinced otherwise, due to his/her past experiences with the particular brand or type of shampoo.

Perceived Risk and Motivation of Skateboarding
by John S. Murphy

Skateboarding is back and this time it shows every indication of becoming a legitimate, professional sport. In the mid 1960s, skateboards were as big and as brief a fad as Hula-Hoops.

A few historical notes: The surfboard was invented by the Hawaiians during the 12th century. The roller skate was invented by an Englishman, Joseph Nerlin, in 1760. Next came the scooter, cheap and homemade, with roller skate wheels on a 2 by 4 and an orange crate up front. Then, in the 1960s five brave California teenagers stayed home from school, turned themselves into "The Beach Boys," and borrowing a guitar pick from Chuck Berry and harmonies from the Everly Brothers, spread the word about surf, sand and girls. In short order, American kids wanted to do what the surfers were doing and on flat, calm days the surfers of southern California had started using skateboards—wooden boards with nailed-on roller-skate wheels, as inland exercise boards (Hiss and Bart 1976).

In 1965, 50 million skateboards were sold and soon piled up in American closets. The problem was that clay wheels, which were preferred by rink skaters because of their speed and used on skateboards, were easily broken, extremely slippery and very unmaneuverable.

Polyurethane wheels and other technological refinements have produced the *comeback* of the skateboard making the new boards safer and far more versatile. Now skateboarding is a $250 million business with its own magazine and professional associations. At least 150 manufacturers are turning out more than 50 models priced from $25 to $70 each. Paragon Sporting Goods at Broadway and 18th Street in New York reported that local skateboard sales soon after they entered the market rose to 50 to 100 skateboards a week.

Perceived Risk.—Skateboard sales can be related to Ted Roselius' (1971) theory of a product's perceived risk. This perceived risk is what the consumer sees as the perceived "cost" of a certain item, which in turn motivates the consumer to invest or not invest in its purchase. This author contends that the perceived risk of buying a skateboard is low—constituting the growing sale and marketing of the skateboard.

First, the time-element risk in purchasing a skateboard is very small. Because a skateboard has few parts and is of simple construction, the probability that the purchase will "not work" is small. Therefore, the potential purchaser can be almost certain that he or she will not have to waste time returning the skateboard.

Second, the price of a skateboard is relatively low, thus making the money-element risk low. Skateboarding is big thrills on a small budget. One doesn't need any more equipment than a board or any more room than a sidewalk. To many skaters it is a perfect all-around athletic involvement, combining many features of several sports (surfing, skiing, dance and gymnastics) and provides great potential for individual expression. For some, skateboards are simply a cheap mode of transportation. Emery Air Freight in Los Angeles has hired two agile boarders to deliver small packages. College students shuttle between classes on skateboards while kids use them to deliver newspapers. One mailman in Long Island gave up his bicycle for a board on his daily route (Kellogg 1976).

Following with this, a third element, the ego-element risk in purchasing a skateboard is low. As stated previously, a skateboard is a very simple device; therefore, a buyer should know exactly what he/she is getting. Whether the skateboard is bought for doing tricks or simply rolling about, the skater's ego will surely rise as he/she gets better and better. Enjoyment itself is capable of raising ego. If someone buys a board for transportation, his or her ego will be strengthened by thoughts of its convenience or its money saving value.

Hazards are the fourth element of perceived risk. In the case of skateboards, the risk of hazard is prevalent. However, with knowledge of skateboarding and taking certain precautions, this author feels that the possible hazards are equal to or below other forms of transportation or recreation. The new polyurethane wheels have cut down on the possibility of injury. The old steel or clay wheels would usually throw a person off the board when encountering even a small pebble. The new wheels handle rough terrain very well. The knowledge that skateboards are now safer is a definite reason for the drastic increase in the skateboard industry over the past year or so.

Motivation.—Arthur Koponen's study of the personality characteristics of purchasers is very useful here. Koponen's study was based on the Edwards' Personal Preference Test, which measures 15 psychological needs (Koponen 1960). These are only needs which an individual expresses, not necessarily how he or she really feels or behaves and may or may not be related to buying behavior.

It has been determined that the skateboard industry caters to the young. Koponen found that the young were high in expressed need for change and exhibition. In the Edwards Test, change is defined as: to do new things, to do different things, to change daily routine, variety and novelty. This sort of change is definitely related to the young's new preference for skateboards. Exhibition is defined as: to be the center of attention, to have others notice you, to make an impression on others, vanity and self-dramatization. A good skateboarder can definitely become the center of attention. Current skateboard stars are definitely making an impression on others.

Skateboarding is a sport for both sexes but it appears that more males than females are turning towards the boards, especially in tougher competition. Two of Koponen's expressed needs for men are relevant to the skateboard industry. The first is achievement which is defined by Edwards as: to rival and surpass, to do one's best, to desire prestige, accomplishment, ambition, success. Skateboarding is made up of all of these, especiallly in head to head competitions where each person wants to prove he/she is the best. Second is dominance which is defined as: to control others, to be a leader in groups, to influence others, control and supervise. It is just such a dominant person who is especially good for the increasing skateboard sales. His or her influence and leadership will be the reason why many people will run out and buy a skateboard.

This author believes that Koponen's findings are especially useful in determining the target market and advertising campaigns for many products. Relevant to the fact that skateboards were first introduced and developed in California, Koponen in his study found that in the western United States the highest expressed need was for change.

What next? Frank Nasworthy (now associated with Bahne Skateboards) is breaking ground for a $600,000, 15 thousand square-foot concrete skatepark in Fort Lauderdale which will feature a pro shop, a game room, and a place where parents can have refreshments while their children skate. Many less elaborate skateparks are springing up throughout the country. Now the talk is that skateboarding will receive status at the 1980 Moscow Olympics!

Maslow's Hierarchy and the Purchase of Vegetables
by Ruth Carus

Since the human being is a wanting animal, behavior can be explained in relation to the individual's search to make life rewarding and meaningful. Maslow (1968) believed that motives for human behavior are innate and arranged in an ascending hierarchy of needs.

At the base of the pyramid are the physiological needs for physical survival which must be met at least to some degree before any other needs become motivationally important. Next come the safety or security needs for order, structure, predictability and a reasonable degree of certainty. Following are belongingness and love needs which are exemplified by desires for a place in the family or other social groups and for intimacy. After this comes the need for self-esteem which includes self-respect, such as the desire for competence, adequacy, achievement, independence and freedom, and esteem from others—the need for recognition and appreciation for what one can do.

If all the previously mentioned needs are adequately satisfied, finally the need of self-actualization becomes dominant. This is the desire to become everything one is capable of becoming and also the need for cognitive understanding.

Although Maslow considers all humans to be capable of self-actualization, apparently only about 1% of the population fully attains this status (Hjelle and Ziegler 1976) with others operating at one of the lower levels or only partially attaining the highest level. Since he did not develop "types," except for his discussions of self-actualizers (Maddi 1976), this author's discussion of the interpretation of consumption behavior in relation to vegetables will be related to each of the need hierarchies.

At the lowest level we will consider vegetables as a source of essential nutrients which the body must have for physical survival, and as a hunger satisfier. If these needs are not adequately provided, the organism will not survive. The person who consumes vegetables because of the nutrients provided or for hunger satiety will be motivated, in part, by this basic-level need. A minimal satisfaction of the basic need can occur due to lack of knowledge, income or lack of perception of an obvious relationship between inadequacy of need-fulfillment (disease) and inadequacy of nutrient intake. An example of this would be the development of vitamin A deficiency symptoms in the tropics where there are potential sources of vitamin A all around.

If the individual perceives a meal as containing meat, starch and a vegetable, then the second level or security needs will be met with the provision of the vegetable. If corned beef and cabbage are expected at the same time, then again the need for order and predictability will motivate the person to eat cabbage when also eating corned beef. The consumption of asparagus in the spring, corn-on-the-cob in summer and pumpkin at Thanksgiving are also tied to the security needs. Davitt and Rotter (1973) related bargain seekers to order needs, so the price conscious, "pick-it-yourself" individual may be motivated by security needs.

The purchasing of items preferred by the group to which one belongs, such as zucchini, tomatoes and garlic by a southern Italian, greens, sweet potatoes and peas (beans) by a southerner and the presentation of liked foods to liked persons would be examples of fulfillment of belongingness and love needs. Where good nutrition and good health are prized, the providing of healthful foods (such as greens, tomatoes, etc.) prepared in healthful ways (raw, cooked to preserve nutrients, or in oil rather than fat) could also be related to love needs as well as to physiological needs.

Self-esteem and other esteem needs would be exemplified by the perception of an individual as a good mother, frugal housekeeper, as an I-hate-to-cook housekeeper, or as one who is known to set a good table. The person who considers spending much time in the kitchen as a waste would be more likely to use canned, frozen, sauced or seasoned or raw vegetables in salads, while the "frugal housekeeper" would use those vegetables which were least expensive, in season, or this person might have a vegetable garden. "Setting a good table" could mean elaborate preparation, expensive and/or out of season products, high quality, great variety and quantity. The closer the person comes to meeting their own or others' ideal, the greater their satisfaction will be.

The self-actualizer would be characterized by the interest in trying new products, using them in different ways, providing them in adequate amounts, understanding something about them, but only accepting for continued contact that which gives satisfaction of "feeling of well-being" or "rightness." In other words, the person would be trying to be creative, individual, knowledgeable and also using the products as a means of contact with others.

Vegetable consumption in its relationship to control of body weight, prevention of heart disease and attainment of general good health could be looked on as satisfying not only basic physiological needs but also as an aspect of providing for safety needs, for love needs (taking care of and being taken care of), self-esteem ("good mother" image, attractiveness) or self-actualization.

An interesting development is the recent popularity of the salad bar, which until recently was only found in more expensive restaurants and was more popular on the west coast. At what level(s) of motivation can this be explained? Has greater knowledge increased the perception of the relationship of vegetables to general health (physiological needs and safety needs)? Has greater sophistication now put it into the "in" category (belongingness and self-esteem)? Is it also an indication of the striving for creativity and perfectibility (self-actualization)? Certainly all components of Maslow's hierarchy for the motivation of human behavior are exemplified in this one aspect of consumer behavior regarding vegetables.

REFERENCES

ADLER, A. 1966. The psychology of power. J. Indiv. Psychol. *22*, 166-172.

ANON. 1976. Shampoos: The detergent in them cleans your hair, but what's the fruit salad for? Consumer Rept. *41*, 617-618.

ASCH, S. 1951. Effects of group pressure on the modification and distortion of judgements. *In* Groups, Leadership and Men (H. Guetzkow, Editor.) Carnegie, Pittsburgh.

BECKER, G. 1976. The Economic Approach to Human Behavior. Univ. of Chicago Press, Chicago.

BROADBENT, D., 1958. Perception and Communication. Pergamon Press, London.

BRUNER, J. and GOODMAN, C. 1947. Value and need as organizing factors in perception. J. Abnormal Soc. Psychol. *42*, 33-44.

CATTELL, R. B. 1959. The dynamic calculus: Concepts and crucial experiments. *In* Nebraska Symp. on Motivation. (R.R. Jones, Editor.) Univ. of Nebraska Press, Lincoln.

DAVITT, C. and ROTTER, G. 1973. Development of a bargain—Interest attitude scale. Psychol. Abstr. *50*, 4905.

DOLLARD, J. and MILLER, N. 1950. Personality and Psychotherapy. McGraw-Hill, New York.

DEUTSCH, J. and DEUTSCH, D. 1963. Attention: Some theoretical considerations. Psychol. Rev. *70*, 80-90

FROMM, E. 1941. Escape from Freedom. Rinehart, New York.

HASTORF, A. and CANTRIL, H. 1954. They saw a game: A case study. J. Abnormal Soc. Psychol. *49*, 129-134.

HISS, T. and BART, S. 1976. Free as a board. N.Y. Times Mag., Sept. 12.

HJELLE, L. A. and ZEIGLER, D. J. 1976. Personality Theories: Basic Assumptions, Research and Applications. McGraw-Hill, N.Y.

HOPKINS, H. C. 1975. And Now A Word About Your Shampoo. U.S. Govnt. Printing Off., Washington, D.C.

HORNEY, K. 1945. Our Inner Conflicts. Norton, New York.

HULL, C. L. 1943. Principles of Behavior. Appleton-Century-Crofts, New York.

KAHNEMAN, D. 1973. Attention and Effort. Prentice-Hall, Englewood Cliffs, New Jersey.

KATONA, G. 1951. Psychological Analysis of Economic Behavior. McGraw-Hill, New York.

KELLOGG, M. A. 1976. Rebirth of the boards. Newsweek, June 21.

KOPONEN, A. 1960. Personality characteristics of purchasers. J. Advertis. Res. *1*, 6-12

KRECH, D. and CRUTCHFIELD, R. 1948. Theory and Problems of Social Psychology. McGraw-Hill, New York.

LANCASTER, K. 1966. A New Approach to Consumer Theory. J. Pol. Econ. *74*, 132-157.

LEUBA, C. and LUCAS, C. 1945. The effects of attitudes on descriptions of pictures. J. Exper. Psychol. *35*, 517-524.

LEVY, L. 1970. Conceptions of Personality: Theories and Research. Random House, New York.

MADDI, S. R., 1976. Personality Theories: A Comparative Analysis. Dorsey Press, Homewood, Ill.

MASLOW, A. 1943. A theory of human motivation. Psychol. Rev. *50*, 370-396.

MASLOW, A. H. 1968. Toward a Psychology of Being. Second Edition. D. Van Nostrand Co., N.Y.

MURRAY, H. A. 1938. Explorations in Personality. Oxford Univ. Press, London.

NEISSER, U. 1976. Cognition and Reality. W.H. Freeman and Co., San Francisco.

NORMAN, D. 1976. Memory and Attention, 2nd ed. John Wiley and Sons, New York.

PERVIN, L. 1975. Personality: Theory, Assessment and Research. Second Edition. John Wiley and Sons, New York.

ROBERTSON, T. S. 1970. Consumer Behavior. Scott, Foresman and Co., Glenview, Ill.

ROGERS, C. 1959. A theory of therapy, personality and interpersonal relationships as developed in the client-centered framework. *In* Psychology: A Study of a Science. Vol. 3. (Sigmund Koch, Editor.) McGraw-Hill, New York.

ROSELIUS, T. 1971. Consumer rankings of risk reduction methods. J. Marktg. *35*.

TRIESMAN, A. 1964. Verbal cues, language and meaning in selective attention. Amer. J. Psychol. *77*, 206-219.

WATERS, H. F. 1977. What television does to kids. Newsweek *89*, 67.

4

Indifference Curves:
Attitudes/Response Sets

The nature of the budget line and the motivational assumptions have been considered. There remains the indifference map, saved for last because of the complexity of factors affecting it.

The indifference map is the set of the person's preferences among the elements on the axes. By saying that a person has certain preferences, we can also say that the person has certain attitudes toward those elements. Most researchers agree that attitudes are learned. Both internal and external factors, such as personality and social influence, can affect these attitudes. If a purely behaviorist view is taken, which does not deal with cognitions, one could say that the person has learned a response set when presented with these elements. This response set could then be interpreted as the person's preference. The person has learned that certain elements give relatively more satisfaction than others and perhaps that some tradeoff is possible between them. For example, a thirsty person may find that lemonade quenches his/her thirst better than water; the person will then have learned to respond with lemonade to a thirst need and as such will have developed a preference for lemonade. On the other hand, perhaps the same thirst-satisfaction would occur with one glass of lemonade or two glasses of water. The person may learn this on occasion when lemonade is unavailable. The indifference curve could reflect this tradeoff. Whichever view one takes, the indifference map implies that a person will have a previously learned disposition to respond with respect to those elements. The exact form of the response will depend on the situation reflected in the budget line.

THE STRUCTURAL APPROACH TO ATTITUDES

For the present, preferences will be considered as sets of attitudes. Several views exist concerning the nature of attitudes. One major view concentrates on their structure, while another investigates the function they serve.

The structural approach, which will be described first, requires a definition of an attitude. According to Rokeach (1968), an attitude is a relatively enduring organization of beliefs around an object or situation predisposing one to respond in some preferential manner. All parts of this definition deserve attention. First, an attitude is relatively enduring. Temporary predispositions are not called attitudes. Attitudes are formed by past experiences, through the mechanisms of learning, and as learned responses should also be fairly consistent over time.

Second, an attitude is an organization of beliefs. This necessitates an examination of the concept of belief. Rokeach defines a belief as any simple proposition, conscious or unconscious, inferred from what a person says or does, capable of being preceded by the phrase "I believe that . . ." Three kinds of beliefs exist. A descriptive belief describes the object of belief as true or false, e.g., "I believe that this book is on my desk." An evaluative belief evaluates the object as good or bad, such as "I believe that this is a good book." A prescriptive belief prescribes a certain action or condition as desirable or undesirable, e.g., "I believe that it would be desirable for me to study from this book for this test."

All three kinds of beliefs carry behavioral implications. If I believe this book is on my desk, I will not look for it in the bookcase. If I believe this is a good book, I may recommend it to another person. If I believe I should study for the test, I will very likely study.

Each belief has three components in itself. The behavioral component has just been described. A belief will also have a cognitive component which represents a person's knowledge, held with varying degrees of certitude, about what is true or false, good or bad, desirable or undesirable (Rokeach 1968). Using the above example, what I know about the location, value or use of the book expresses the cognitive components. In addition, there will be an affective component. One could conceivably become somewhat emotional over a belief concerning a book, for example, if someone labeled a book as "trash" which was highly regarded or in which some personal interest was at stake.

Beliefs are organized into attitudes. This implies some dimensions of organization. According to Rokeach (1968), these dimensions can describe not only the organization of beliefs into attitudes, but also that of attitudes into larger attitudinal systems.

One major dimension, differentiation, also implies integration vs segregation. Differentiation refers to the number of parts within an attitude, to the complexity of the attitude. This implies an integration of the differentiated parts by recognizing the similarities among the different parts. Parts which are not integrated are segregated or compartmentalized. This may occur when the person does not perceive a relationship between parts or an inconsistency between them. For example, a student taking a course may have one attitude toward the teacher of a course, another toward the course material and another toward the work required. These are differentiated parts of the general attitude toward the course. If the student likes the teacher, detests the course material, but sees the teacher as having no power to change the course material, the student has segregated these attitudes. The classic examples concerning compartmentalized attitudes are those concerning minority group relations. A person may express favorable attitudes toward members of a minority group but object when they move next door.

Another dimension is centrality. The more central or the more important parts within the organization will more strongly resist change. If they do change, this will have greater effect on other parts than would a change in the more peripheral parts. If a person's attitude toward work contains a central belief that hard work builds character, and a more peripheral belief that working harder brings more money, a change in the first belief would have relatively greater impact on the person's attitude toward work. The person probably would not value work as highly as before. If the second belief changed but the first did not, the person would probably still continue to have a favorable attitude toward work.

Other possible dimensions include (1) time perspectives, e.g., whether the person's beliefs apply to only a given time period or hold for all time; (2) specificity or generality, dealing with the extent to which a person can predict one belief or attitude from another within the same organization, e.g., if a person is prejudiced against one minority group, will he/she be prejudiced against another; and (3) the breadth or narrowness of the attitude, referring to the range of phenomena the attitude covers.

Attitudes are organized around an object or situation. The organization must have some focus. Although traditionally the attitude toward an object has received the most attention, an object is always encountered within some situation about which the person will also have some organized attitude. According to Rokeach (1968), the failure of researchers to recognize this has led to many unsuccessful attempts to predict behavior on the basis of only the attitude toward a single object; these unsuccessful attempts, in turn, have resulted in unjustified conclusions that attitudes and behaviors are often inconsistent.

THE FUNCTIONAL APPROACH TO ATTITUDES

The structural approach thus focuses on the components of an attitude and the organization of these components. These are involved in the structuralist definition of an attitude. Before one turns to the correspondence of attitudes with behaviors, which has been investigated largely by the structuralists, a few more views on the formation of attitudes deserve mention.

Attitudes serve functions for an individual as well as contain a structure. While Katz (1960) does not disagree with the above-described structure of attitudes, he is more interested in the dynamics of attitude formation. Katz defined the functional approach simply as the attempt to understand the reasons people hold the attitudes they do. He groups the functions which attitudes perform for the person according to their motivational basis. As such, these functions relate strongly not only to motivational theory but to personality, which will be described subsequently as a major factor affecting attitudes.

Katz considers four functions which attitudes may serve: adjustment, ego-defensive, value expressive and knowledge. The adjustment or utilitarian function refers to the maximization of utility. People seek to maximize their rewards and minimize the penalties incurred. They develop favorable attitudes toward objects which satisfy their needs and unfavorable attitudes toward objects which have unpleasant consequences. These attitudes are learned through past experience; however developed, they form the person's present preferences. These attitudes may change if they no longer provide the previous level of satisfaction and another attitude would serve better, or if the person has new needs or aspirations. If a new style of dress is more flattering to a woman than the old style, she will change her attitudes toward both the old and new styles. If she has previously been satisfied with looking neat and clean but now wants to look sensational, her attitudes toward clothes will change due to the change in her level of aspiration.

The ego-defensive function is to protect the person's self-image. For example, an unfavorable attitude toward a deodorant may be because a person cannot believe he/she smells bad enough to need one. Freudian defense mechanisms fall under the category of ego-defensive functions. Further discussion of personality theories will be postponed to the next section, but the defense mechanisms serve as examples of how personality may affect attitudes. The changing of ego-defensive attitudes is generally the province of psychotherapists.

Value-expressive attitudes, as the name implies, give expression to the person's values, beliefs and self-image. In particular, research has been done with congruency of consumers' attitudes toward small vs large cars, or toward different models of cars, with their self-image. Jacobson and Kossoff (1963), for example, found that owners of small cars saw themselves as "cautious conservatives," while the owners of large cars saw themselves as "confident explorers." The attitudes toward the cars may change if the person is dissatisfied with his/her self-concept or finds that another attitude would better express it.

The knowledge function has been mentioned previously in the perceptual context. The person will seek organization and meaning in the environment. An attitude which serves this function may change with new information or a change in the environment.

Again, these attitudes have been learned or acquired through other mechanisms. The importance here is that they presently exist and the individual will base his/her decision in part on these present attitudes.

THE INFORMATION PROCESSING APPROACH TO ATTITUDES

A third approach to the study of attitudes, that of information processing (McGuire 1972), will be mentioned briefly as it comprises a significant school of thought on attitude formation and as it parallels mechanisms discussed earlier. Actually, this approach more properly belongs under attitude change, but it does refer to the formation of present attitudes.

Under this approach, attitude formation takes place by a series of six behavioral steps. First, a message is presented which presumably has relevance for attitudes and behavior. Second, given the availability of the message in the world of stimuli, the person must pay attention to it. This involves the selective perception discussed earlier. Third, given that the person has attended to the message, he/she must then comprehend it. Next, the person must yield to it if his/her attitude is to be affected. The status of the communicator(s) and the nature of the communication and its presentation may affect yielding. This yielding must then be retained over time to produce the attitude. Finally, the person presumably will eventually emit behavior in accordance with the attitude.

ATTITUDES AND BEHAVIOR

The nature of attitudes through various approaches has been considered. The next question to consider is whether attitudes in fact have any impact on a person's behavior. Under basic economic theory it was seen how different preference structures may yield different choices. Does the same finding emerge in attitude research?

There seems to be little disagreement on the general theory of the relationship between attitude and behavior. The structural approach to attitudes appears to be the most widely used framework. Virtually every researcher has his/her own set of theoretical terms, but the terms are nearly equivalent. There is also some disagreement on intervening variables between the attitude toward an object and the behavior toward the object, such as whether beliefs, values and behavioral intentions are separate components of attitude or intervening variables. This revolves around the research problem of the definition of attitude. Except for one study (Ajzen and Fishbein 1970), it hasn't made a significant amount of difference in the research. Most of the other researchers dealing with behavior do not separate beliefs or behavioral intentions from attitude. This is not necessarily an inconsistency, perhaps just a difference in fineness of distinctions.

The studies concerning the relationship between attitude and behavior seem to fit under the general formulation expressed by Rokeach (1967). Overt behavior with respect to an object is a function of both the person's attitude toward the object and the person's attitude toward the situation in which he/she is behaving, weighted according to the perceived importance of each of these attitudes.

Attitudes affect a person's behavior in direct proportion to their perceived relative importance; i.e., the more central or the more important the attitude, the more effect it should have on the person's behavior. Most studies have concentrated on measuring the person's attitude toward the object, in the belief that this is the more important attitude. They attempt to either decompose that attitude into cognitive beliefs, affect and behavioral intentions (a division with which others take issue) or, more often, place constraints on that attitude in the form of situational variables. Other studies, especially some of the more recent ones (for example, Wicker 1971) propose that the situational attitudes are more important and in fact can explain more variance than attitudes toward objects. Still other studies attempt to reconcile the poor empirical relationship between attitudes and behavior by suggesting refinements in concepts and measurements (Fishbein and Ajzen 1972; Rokeach 1967; Linn 1965).

Researchers have found little direct relationship between the attitude toward an object and the person's overt behavior toward it without the addition of situational variables. A classic study (LaPiere 1934) compared the negative verbal attitudes the restaurant and motel owners expressed toward serving a Chinese couple with the positive behavior expressed when a Chinese couple actually arrived.

One intervening variable proposed to explain this discrepancy refers to the stability of the verbal attitude. Linn (1965) studied college students who expressed the liberal attitudes of the college subculture but who were raised with discriminatory attitudes and behavior. When tested, these students reverted to the behavior of their upbringing. Linn held that discrepant behavior in a negative direction (liberal attitude and discriminatory behavior) will increase if the liberal attitudes are unstable, through lack of testing and experiences with challenges, and if social involvement is high with the attitudinal object, which brings in a situational variable. Conversely, discrepant behavior in a positive direction (prejudiced attitude and nondiscriminatory behavior) will increase if social involvement level is low and if prejudice is not overtly tested. Festinger (1964) also mentions that a momentary change in verbal attitude accomplished through a persuasive communication will be unstable unless other behavioral change is brought about to support the attitude change. As such, researchers have decomposed the attitude toward an object into the verbal attitude toward the object and the stability of this attitude.

Attitude toward the situation or environment for the behavior has most frequently been separated into social involvement with the attitude object and social constraint imposed by reference group considerations due to the visibility of the behavior. Warner and DeFleur (1969) investigated contingent consistency, i.e., consistency between verbal attitude and behavior, contingent upon social constraint or social visibility of action and social distance. The findings of their research were supported by similar research conducted by Green (1972). Briefly stated, the findings were that the willingness of whites to pose for pictures with blacks was negatively related to the degree of intimacy shown, positively related to attitude toward blacks, and negatively related to the exposure the pictures would have. This could be reformulated and generalized so that overt positive behavior is negatively related to social involvement, positively related to verbal attitude, and negatively related to social constraint.

Ajzen and Fishbein (1970) proposed an algebraic model along the same lines: $B \sim BI = (A\text{-act}) w_0 + (NBs) w_1$. Behavior highly correlates with behavioral intentions which is a weighted additive function of attitude toward the act and social normative beliefs. The only way behavior can change is through a change in one of these constructs. Ajzen and Fishbein assumed a high correlation between behavioral intentions and behavior; however, they added that this correlation would be lower the more general the behavioral intention and the longer the time interval between intention and behavior. This model is consistent with the other studies. Ajzen and Fishbein (1970) also tested the inclusion of situational variables against having only the attitude-toward-act variable and found that attitudinal variables did not suffice for prediction while attitudinal with situational variables did.

Wicker (1971) focused his attention on various relevant situational variables and their relative importance. In studying the relation between church members' attitudes toward the church and their behavior with respect to the church, attitude toward the church ranked third in importance behind the situational variables of the judged influence of extraneous events such as good weather, visiting relatives, etc., on church behavior and the more specific attitudes toward the behaviors measured. The last-mentioned influence led Wicker to recommend refocusing the attitude measure from the object to the specific behavior studied, as well as assessing variables other than attitude. In this conclusion, other researchers (Fishbein and Ajzen 1972; Fishbein 1967) agree.

The general framework of the relationship between attitude and behavior seems pretty well agreed upon. Nearly all studies done seem to concern various facets of Rokeach's framework. Behavior depends on attitude-toward-object and attitude-toward-situation. Attitude-toward-object involves the verbal attitude and the stability of the attitude; attitude-toward-situation involves social involvement and social constraint. Theories on attribution, discussed under attitude change, also use the general form of behavior as a function of both attitudinal and situational variables, although attribution theory works in the opposite direction of causation or inference from these studies. Even the main components of situational variables, social involvement and constraint remain fairly constant from study to study, although this seems to be more by accident than by design.

What are not generally agreed upon are the precise definitions of the basic concepts, such as attitudes. It is fairly clear, though, that the various researchers have basically the same ideas in mind. Research methods of many studies in this line cited by Fishbein and Ajzen (1972) are not faultless methodologically. Experimenter bias is evident. For example, nearly all the experiments concerned race relations and attempts to induce liberal attitudes or behavior. Other problems include variables not held constant and low percentages of variance explained, which are common to most psychological studies. Still, there appears to be a tacitly agreed upon, or stumbled upon, as the case may be, theory concerning the structure of attitudes and their relationship to behavior.

As indicated before, the indifference-curve analysis refers to the elements on the axes in the particular situation. This removes the attitude-toward-situation factor which was the major qualification to the relationship between attitude-toward-object and behavior with respect to the object. Therefore, considerable empirical support exists for the relationship between attitudes, as reflected in the indifference map and the person's choice.

APPLICATION OF THEORIES

Information Processing and Cereal Advertising
by Barbara Herondorf

The cereal industry recognizes the fact that a great many people like something sweet for breakfast, especially children, and they have catered to our likes. Clever advertising is the basis for the success of the industry and the fact that a "good breakfast to start the day" is important, is promoted.

McGuire's (1972) information processing approach is useful in explaining how advertising is effective. An advertisement for "King Vitaman," which appeared in *Ladies Home Journal* in 1974, is a good example to use in explaining this theory.

The advertisement depicts a young mother, Mrs. Nancy Kay Condylis, and her daughter, 10-year old Shawn Condylis, posed with the mother's hands on the daughter's shoulders. The mother's long skirt is of the same material as the daughter's jumper. They are sitting in a comfortable room with a shag rug, plants and plenty of light shining through the windows in the background.

In the upper right hand corner, the advertisement reads:

"Does working interfere with being a mother?"

And Mrs. Nancy Kay Condylis answers: "Our family has always been very close. But my working has added something. It's made me a more interesting person to Shawn. It's helped her understand the value of pursuing something you want and enjoy, and seems to make it easier for her to express her own ideas. I like that."

And Quaker Oats tells us in the lower right hand corner: "If you're going to buy her a children's cereal, buy the most nourishing. This [King Vitaman] is the only children's cereal that meets government standards for a vitamin and iron supplement."

First, the message is presented.

Second, the consumer must pay attention to the message. Here we see a picture of an attractive mother with her arms around her daughter. Notice both have matching dresses. They are sitting in the living room of what does not appear to be a low income family. The mother's philosophical statement at the top of the page reveals that she is a working mother who wants a close relationship with her daughter. This ad will get attention because it is one that most mothers can relate to.

Third, the consumer must understand the message. The message is easily understandable and aimed towards the housewife who has one or more children. (The *Ladies Home Journal* is a magazine aimed towards the housewife.) The advertiser is trying to get the point across that the mother loves her little girl and wants only the best for her, so she buys her daughter only the best cereal, "the only cereal that meets government standards."

Fourth, the consumer must yield to the message and believes it. The reader must be influenced by this message. This author doubts that this ad would be successful in a sports car magazine or in *Cosmopolitan*, since the types of readers of these two magazines would not predominately be the loving mother pictured in this ad. The reader must believe that King Vitaman is the best or one of the best cereals on the market, and is, therefore, influenced into buying the product.

Fifth, the reader must retain the belief over time. This refers to the fact that after being emotionally influenced by the ad, the reader must remember the ad and be influenced enough so that she will actually want to buy the product when she gets to the store.

Sixth, the reader will produce behavior that corresponds to the message. After the reader has been presented with the message, pays attention to it, comprehends and relates the message presented, believes the message, and remembers it when she gets to the store, will she actually buy the product? Quaker manufacturers hope she will.

Will the mother buy King Vitaman when she gets to the store? People don't always do what they say they will or what they intend to—that is, their verbal attitude toward an object may not be stable or their attitudes toward the situation may outweigh it. When the mother gets to the grocery store, she may buy another product. Why?

(1) Does she feel King Vitaman is the *best* breakfast food she can buy or will she buy oatmeal which she feels is better than King Vitaman?

(2) Cost may influence her decision after she sees that King Vitaman is 40¢ more a box than Trix, the cereal she has been buying. Is King Vitaman so much better than Trix that she will be willing to pay the extra money?

(3) Advertisers use "come-on" gimmicks such as free samples, trading stamps, money-back guarantees, gifts at reducd prices, free gifts, and coupons in an attempt to change behavior. It is hoped that these gimmicks will

influence a customer to buy their product. Will she buy Buc Wheats instead of King Vitaman because she has a 7¢ coupon?

(4) Many mothers take their children with them while they shop. Will the child influence her mother to buy the cereal with Fred Flintstone on the box or the green and blue cereal instead of King Vitaman?

Regardless of which cereal she buys, the industry wins. Most of the manufacturers have more than one brand of cereal. So, if she decides to buy Buc Wheats, put out by Quaker, instead of oatmeal by Quaker, Quaker has still made a sale.

REFERENCES

AJZEN, I. and FISHBEIN, M. 1971. The prediction of behavior from attitudinal and normative variables. J. Exper. Soc. Psychol. *6*, 466-487.

FESTINGER, L. 1964. Behavioral support for opinion change. Public Opinion Quart. *30*, 529-550.

FISHBEIN, M. 1967. Attitude and the prediction of behavior. *In* Readings in Attitude Theory and Measurement. (M. Fishbein, Editor.) John Wiley and Sons, New York.

FISHBEIN, M. and AJZEN, I. 1972. Attitudes and opinions. Ann. Rev. Psychol. *23*. 487-544.

GREEN, J. 1972. Attitudinal and situational determinants of intended behavior toward blacks. J. Personality Soc. Psychol. *22*, 13-17.

JACOBSEN, E. and KOSSOFF, J. 1963. Self-percept and consumer attitudes toward small cars. J. Applied Psychol. *47*, 242-245.

KATZ, D. 1960. The functional approach to the study of attitudes. Public Opinion Quart. *24*, 163-294.

LAPIERE, R. 1934. Attitudes vs actions. Social Forces *13*, 230-237.

LINN, L. 1965. Verbal attitudes and overt behavior-study of racial discrimination. Social Forces *43*, 353-364.

McGUIRE, W. 1972. Attitude change: The information processing paradigm. Experimental Social Psychology. (C. McClintock, Editor.) Holt, Rinehart and Winston, New York.

ROKEACH, M. 1967. Attitude change and behavior change. Public Opinion Quart. *30*, 529-550.

ROKEACH, M. 1968. Beliefs, Attitudes and Values. Jossey-Bass, San Francisco.

WARNER, L. and DEFLEUR, M. 1969. Attitude as interactional concept: Constraint and social distance as intervening variables between attitudes and actions. Amer. Sociol. Rev. *34*, 153-169.

WICKER, A. 1971. An examination of the "other variables" explanation of attitude-behavior inconsistency. J. Personality Soc. Psychol. *19*, 18-30.

5

Factors Affecting
Attitudes: Personality

The indifference curve map reflects the person's attitudes and/or response sets toward the items on the axes and these attitudes' effects on behavior. Several views on the determinants, functions and/or components of these attitudes have been discussed. Two major kinds of factors which affect a person's attitudes, those of personality and social influence, remain.

CATTELL'S FACTOR ANALYTIC APPROACH

Cattell (1959) proposed that behavior depends on both personality traits and the situation. This resembles both Rokeach's delineation of attitude toward the object and attitude toward the situation and the thesis proposed here of indifference curves, reflecting preferences and situational constraints. According to Cattell, one could conceivably pinpoint exactly how much influence each factor has on a given behavior through what he terms a specification equation. A small number of traits should account for a large part of human behavior. Further, some traits typically characterize some situations. Therefore, by putting traits and the situation together, one should be able to predict behavior fairly well in a typical situation.

Cattell's approach is notable because he derived his theory entirely from data. He started with data collection, then factor analyzed the data to see what major factors emerged that could account for most of the data. While his exclusive reliance on factor analysis as a theoretical tool has been questioned, his theoretical results seem to concur with those of other theorists. His work has particular value to the extent that it yields the same results as others while approaching the subject from an entirely different direction. This has already been discussed to some degree in examining theories of motivation.

Cattell's traits can be described in various ways, as dynamic (motivational) or static (characteristic), source (underlying) or surface (superficial), constitutional (hereditary tendencies) or environmental mold (learned) traits. Cattell focuses on the dynamic source traits in which heredity and learning interact. These have three major components:

(1) *Attitude*: The person expresses an attitude in the form of "under these circumstances, I want this much to do *this*." Attitudes are numerous; their importance lies in their collective representation of the interaction of a relatively small number of ergs and sentiments. As mentioned above, attitudes are reflected in the person's indifference map.

(2) *Erg*: Ergs represent the person's hereditary motivational tendencies. In Cattell's terms, they become the constitutional dynamic source traits. They occupy roughly the same position in Cattell's theory that the concepts of instinct and primary drive have in other theories; however, Cattell inferred his ergs from his empirical work. He empirically separated the proportions of variance attributable to heredity and environment, e.g., by comparing differences between identical and fraternal twins. He emerged with a set of nine to eleven ergs, i.e., traits heavily influenced by heredity, including sex, gregariousness, parental protectiveness, curiosity, general fear, self-assertion, self-oriented sensuality, aggressiveness and constructiveness. These are not necessarily Cattell's labels for the ergs but should indicate the approximate meaning.

The intensity of the ergs varies with both the person and the occasion. Their dimensions include (a) their drive strength, which refers to the heredity excitation level the person has; (b) the need strength, that is, the person's state of physiological deprivation at that point in time; and (c) the person's current level of stimulation. Variations in ergic tension (intensity) exist, therefore, according to the person's heredity makeup, his/her past experience which contributes to need at present, and the stimulation offered by the present occasion. These ergs are then expressed as a set of attitudes.

(3) *Sentiment*: As the ergs represent the person's constitutional dynamic source traits, so the sentiments represent his/her environmental mold dynamic source traits. These are social in nature, e.g., a home sentiment is a set of related attitudes toward home and family life. As ergs relate to a person's primary (biological) drives, sentiments relate to secondary (learned, social) drives. Sentiments do not develop without the influence of one or more ergs; they are learned on the basis of ergs. In this connection, Cattell's theory resembles learning theory which will be discussed subsequently. Other examples of sentiments include career (similar to an achievement motivation), religion, interest in mechanics, spouse/sweetheart, social desirability, patriotism and self.

The self sentiment is centrally important. It reflects the person's attitudes toward him/herself and often becomes a question of self-liking. Virtually every other attitude filters through this one. Cattell's self-sentiment strongly resembles concepts in other personality theories, especially that of Rogers who makes the self-concept a major theoretical construct.

The relationships among ergs, sentiments and attitudes take on a hierarchical ordering. The ergs are the most basic and the most important. Sentiments are based on ergs. Attitudes can be based on either ergs or sentiments or some combination of the two.

Cattell's concept for integrating the components, the dynamic lattice, is the set of all interrelationships among ergs, sentiments and attitudes for a given individual. The lattice shows which traits are closely associated with each other. This pattern among the traits, will vary greatly with the individual. The form of this integrative system does not greatly differ from those found in other theories, such as Freud's id-ego-superego triad, although obviously the substance of the theories differs. The lattice is also fairly stable over time. Ergs change only as their (relatively small) environmental component is influenced by changes in the environment. Sentiments can be considered as

essentially well-established habit patterns, which also will change but slowly, and attitudes (based on the ergs and sentiments) can change but in general tend to be stable.

Cattell's theory has been discussed first because it encompasses a broad range of both theoretical and empirical phenomena and because it has aspects similar to several other theories while approaching the subject matter from a strictly empirical basis.

EYSENCK'S FACTOR ANALYTIC APPROACH

Eysenck (1953) focused on the biological basis of personality. Working independently from Cattell, although also starting with empirical data and factor analysis, Eysenck came up with major personality dimensions of extroversion/introversion, neuroticism (actually a measure of emotional volatility) and psychoticism. Cattell also found extroversion and neuroticism when he factor analyzed his original data. Eysenck has traced extroversion and neuroticism to neurological functioning, especially arousal.

In particular, he has tied extroversion/introversion to cortical inhibition/excitation. An increase in cortical inhibition results in less control exerted (via the cortex) over the functions, which generally results in extroverted behavior. Conversely, an increase in cortical excitation results in more control over other functions, which leads to introverted behavior. A person will have a certain balance of the two processes of excitation and inhibition. While this balance at the cortical level changes with the situation, each individual has a certain operating level of it which leads to a general pattern of extroverted or introverted behavior. Extroversion/introversion, in turn, has certain other behavioral patterns associated with it (e.g., introverts condition more easily to weak stimuli than do extroverts), which carry further implications for the given person's behavior. Studies conducted with identical vs fraternal twins support the notion of genetic basis for the neurophysiological balance between excitation and inhibition. The chain of reasoning then becomes: differences in this balance result in differences in behavior. There

is a neurophysiological basis for these balance differences. Since genetic basis for the neurophysiological differences exists, there is a genetic basis for behavior.

Less research has been done concerning the neuroticism dimension, and still less on psychoticism. Neuroticism appears to be related to the limpic system in the brain, which controls the person's emotional responses. While extroversion relates to the person's overall arousal level, neuroticism involves a much more specific type of arousal, that is, emotional arousal. This is one of many inputs into overall general arousal, although in some situations the emotional arousal is so strong that it overrides the other components of general arousal. Although this indirect relationship between extroversion and neuroticism exists, statistically they appear to be independent.

Both Eysenck's and Cattell's theories (with developed questionnaires) were applied in investigating marijuana use among high school girls (Robinson 1970). The Eysenck Personality Inventory showed marked differences between smokers and nonsmokers along the extroversion dimension. Smokers were more extroverted than established norms while nonsmokers were more introverted than average. This concurs with Eysenck's implications that introverts condition more readily than do extroverts. In this case, social conditioning should discourage smoking. Both smokers and nonsmokers scored fairly high on the neuroticism dimension, but did not significantly differ from each other.

Robinson also used a modification of Cattell's 16 personality factor questionnaire which was developed for junior-senior high school students. The findings on smokers vs nonsmokers indicated that smokers were relatively more socially group dependent, more conventional, more out-going, less dependable, more impulsive, self-indulgent and self-assured than were nonsmokers. This research supports the notion that personality traits are related to consumption behavior.

Cattell and Eysenck have been in the minority of twentieth century psychologists in their attention to biological and hereditary bases for personality and resulting attitudes and behavior. Most psychological literature emphasizes the role of the environment in shaping a person's personality and behavior. This point of view reflects the old idea of the tabula rasa—the blank slate on which experience writes.

The essentials of the psychoanalytical approach have already been described under theories of motivation. The Freudian school has obtained more respect for its influence on later psychological thought than for its usefulness in research. One of the neoanalytical theories, that of Karen Horney, will be discussed as an example of neoFreudian thought and because consumer research has been done based directly on this theory.

HORNEY'S NEOANALYTICAL APPROACH

Horney (1945) takes a more holistic approach than does Cattell. Rather than merely listing a number of traits, she combines them into three clusters representing three possible predominant social orientations of individuals. Basically, these are moving toward people (compliant), moving against people (aggressive) and moving away from people (detached). Each orientation involves a different pattern of dealing with other individuals.

The compliant individual has a great desire to be loved and needs to belong with others. As a result, this person may become oversensitive to the needs of others, overconsiderate and overgenerous. In the desire for love and acceptance, the person will downgrade his/her own needs and wishes for the sake of other peoples'. The compliant person wishes to avoid interpersonal conflict and as a result is reluctant to criticize others and willing to take the blame him/herself. This person is generally a strong conformist in behavior, since social acceptance has such importance for him or her.

The aggressive person has a strong desire to excell, to achieve success, prestige and admiration. This person sees other people as competitors for this prestige and reacts to them accordingly. The aggressive person needs people, not as the compliant person does, but to reinforce his/her self-image. This person will likely be a nonconformist because this way he/she will acquire attention providing that the attention is of an admiring variety.

The detached person has little interest in other people. In fact, the distinguishing characteristic of the detached person is a desire to put emotional distance between him/herself and others. This person values independence and self-sufficiency and may be distrustful of other people. Some individuals may eventually select this orientation as a result of negative experiences with both compliant and aggressive strategies.

The individual will tend to select one predominant strategy which has given him/her the most satisfaction in previous experiences, e.g., as child dealing with parents. The particular strategy selected will depend on not only this previous reinforcement for various strategies but on how appropriate the person perceives each type of behavior for a given situation. For example, if a person's parents only rewarded the child when he/she did something well, such as bringing home straight-A report cards, the child may develop an aggressive orientation. However, the person as an adult may not behave in this way in all situations. For instance, aggressiveness may be perceived as appropriate behavior for on-the-job situations but not for relating to a spouse. Still, the personality classification refers to a general orientation.

Cohen (1967) has found Horney's theory to be relevant to consumer market behavior. A person will purchase many products, such as personal grooming products, to help him/her achieve goals which involve other people or to make a statement about him/herself to others. The compliant person will desire the security of being liked and as such is a heavier consumer of mouthwash and certain brands of soap and deodorant which are advertised with an interpersonal appeal. The aggressive person, in establishing a unique identity, will prefer more distinctive brands. The detached person is not overly concerned with the purchase of personal grooming products, as he/she is not so concerned with other people's reactions. To return for a moment to economic theory, obviously the budget line should not vary systematically with personality type unless one considers perceived social risk for the compliant person. The difference in behavior must come from the difference in indifference maps, which concern relative attitudes toward the products and which as seen here are affected by the individual's personality type.

DOLLARD AND MILLER: THE SOCIAL LEARNING APPROACH

Learning theory itself will be discussed after considering what happens after the person makes his/her choice. However, previous learning will affect the present choice. Besides the informational aspect considered with the budget line, a person can learn attitudes and personality traits. Cattell indicated that learning affects a certain set of traits, the "sentiments." Another school of personality theorists, including Dollard and Miller (1950), holds that personality itself is learned. This view sees the human as the blank slate, so environment is of vital importance. Personality becomes the structure of a complex set of habits; habits are the learned associations between stimulus and response.

The basic elements of this theory are drive, cue, response and reinforcement. Drives, or needs, are strong motivating stimuli. They may be innate (primary, physiological, such as hunger and thirst) or learned (secondary, such as achievement and social status). A person acquires the learned drives on the basis of the innate drives.

Drives impel responses of some sort. What kind of response the person makes is directed by a cue. Cues are weaker stimuli which guide the form of the response. For example, a person may be thirsty: an innate drive. The person may satisfy thirst in a number of ways or by a number of products. A cola advertisement may provide the cue for the response to drink a cola.

The response obviously is whatever the person does. Responses may also be innate, such as reflexes, or learned. The person has a hierarchy of responses available and could make any of several responses to a given stimulus. Some responses will be preferred over others, i.e., drinking a cola vs drinking water, although the latter may still be used if the former is unavailable or does not work to the person's satisfaction. Previous learning will heavily influence the ordering of this hierarchy.

Reinforcement is whatever increases the probability that a particular response will be made to a particular stimulus. Intuitively, this includes the satisfaction the person derives from making the response. According to Dollard and Miller, only events which reduce the initiating drives are reinforcing. In the cola example, if drinking the cola reduces the person's thirst, that reaction to thirst is reinforced and the person has an increased likelihood of drinking a cola the next time he/she is thirsty.

Dollard and Miller broadened this traditional learning approach to include social learning. The person learns responses to social stimuli and thereby forms habits which constitute his/her personality. Whether one wants to consider these as cognitions or response sets depends on how behaviorist a view one takes. Social learning theory also offered alternative explanations to some psychoanalytic phenomena; for example, Dollard and Miller's interpretation of the unconscious as a set of automated habits of which the person need no longer be aware. Some material may have become unconscious by having been learned before the person has the verbal symbols to express it. Dollard and Miller explain repression which is the forcing of material out of consciousness as a learning mechanism. The stopping of anxiety-arousing thoughts reduces anxiety and therefore repression is reinforced. The learning approach to personality, then, seems to offer an alternative to the more traditional personality theories in explaining the same phenomena. Either approach will support the purposes of the present indifference-curve argument.

BANDURA AND WALTERS: OBSERVATIONAL LEARNING

Even the learning approach has its variations. Observational learning theory developed as a result of limitations which Bandura and Walters (1963) perceived in traditional learning theory. In particular, in the traditional stimulus-response-reinforcement model a response must first somehow be made in order to be reinforced and learned. Except through the later-added mechanism of generalization, there was no way to account for new behaviors. Also, the behaviors may not be observed for some time after the period of learning and they appeared to be acquired without reinforcement having necessarily occurred. To illustrate the latter point, one does not have to put one's hand in the fire to know that the fire is hot. Bandura stated that the provision of social models is an indispensable means of transmitting and modifying behavior in situations where errors are likely to produce costly or fatal consequences. Further, if the process of social learning proceeded exclusively on the basis of rewarding and punishing consequences, most people would never survive the socialization process.

Bandura holds then that people can learn merely by observing the behavior of others. Reinforcement is not necessarily part of the learning process. Obviously, the types of behavior considered in this theory are the imitative and identifying behaviors involved in social learning.

The critical distinction in this theory is between the acquisition and performance of behavior. In the early research (see Bandura 1965), children who observed the model being rewarded for aggressive behavior would reproduce the model's behavior, while those who saw the model being punished would not perform that behavior. However, even those who did not perform the behavior could describe it accurately. This occurred when the children had not been given any incentive to perform or not to perform the behavior themselves. When given such incentives, all children performed the aggressive behavior. This suggests that reinforcement to the model for the aggressive behavior affected the children's spontaneous performance of that behavior but not the learning of it.

Although most of the research has concerned children's imitation of an adult, adults are hypothesized to learn by observation also. For example, consider the purchase of a new style of boots. If a friend buys the new style and receives compliments, the observer is likely to try the new style also. The observer has not yet received any reinforcement; the model has. If the boots are unattractive and do nothing for the friend's appearance, the observer may not buy the boots him/herself but he/she has acquired the information that the boots exist, are purchasable and are unattractive.

Not all observers will necessarily follow the model. This will depend on the characteristics of the model, i.e., prestige of the model and of the observer, i.e., dependency. Also, the behavior considered must be distinctive enough to attract the observer's attention and must have aspects that can be communicated to and by the observer. For example, one cannot easily reproduce the behavior of an opera singer.

Observational learning involves four major processes (Bandura 1971). First are attentional processes. If the observer does not attend to the model, he/she will not likely adopt the model's behavior. Second are retentional processes. The observer notices significant aspects of the model's behavior and must retain what he/she sees, i.e., by the symbolic encoding of the features of the model's behavior. The observer may do this encoding through either words or mental images. So far, the processes postulated are consistent with those involved in information processing described earlier.

The third set of processes are those of motoric reproduction, that is, behavior. People may learn many things that they never express but which they have available in their repertoires. A person may never have shot a gun but may know how to pull the trigger. As yet, there has been no mention made of reinforcement; modeling can take place without reinforcement.

Finally come the motivational and reinforcement processes. Reinforcement can be an important condition for the expression of behavior which has been learned through modeling. The behavior has been learned or acquired without reinforcement; the expression or performance of the behavior may be affected by reinforcement. The reinforcement need not be to the observer; in fact, nearly all of the reinforcement considered in observational learning is to the model.

Exposure to modeling then can result in the acquisition of new responses, the inhibition (via negative reinforcement to model) of the expression of behavior, or the elicitation of behavior presently existing in the person's repertoire.

Observational learning contributes to explanation of personality and the development of a response set of attitudes in much the same way that straight stimulus-response-reinforcement learning does. In addition to learning of behaviors, the person may learn values and emotional reactions. Research concerning the learning of aggression, moral judgements, the setting of moral and social standards, vicarious conditioning of fears, delay of gratification (Bandura and Mischel 1965) and altruism has been done. In particular, differences in values for deferred gratification affect the differential use of credit cards (Mathews and Slocum 1969). This supports the link between learned attitudes and subsequent behavior. Differences in the effectiveness of different types of models have also been explored. For the purposes of the present argument, it is the acquired but not necessarily yet performed values and preferences which would affect the indifference map on the basis of which the person would then behave.

ROGERS: HUMANISTIC

Entirely different from the learning approach is the view of Carl Rogers (1959). His is a highly humanistic theory of personality focusing on how the person experiences the environment and him/herself. Rogers focuses on the person's consciousness as opposed to the emphasis on the unconscious by the psychoanalytic school. A key element in Rogers' theory is that of the self. At birth the human organism has only a few relevant hereditary properties. Primary among these is the motive of actualization which was discussed earlier. The person will also have a screening mechanism, termed the organismic valuing process, which evaluates each experience as to whether it will further the actualization process and, therefore, should be repeated in the future.

One of the functions of actualization is differentiation, also previously mentioned. The conscious self will differentiate out of the total organism and self-actualization out of actualization. Learned "conditions of worth" parallel the organismic valuing process in serving as the screening mechanism for the self. The conditions of worth evaluate each experience as to whether it enhances the self-concept, whether it be favorable or unfavorable. Consistent experiences are stored in awareness; inconsistent experiences are stored out of awareness. This has no relation to the organismic valuing process. For example, an experience may be beneficial for actualization but inconsistent with the existing self-concept. The person either would not be aware of this beneficial experience which should be repeated, or would distort the experience in accordance with the existing self-concept. For instance, a poor student may attribute an A on a test to luck rather than alter his/her self-concept of a poor student. This impedes the organism's growth. Rogers' focus of therapy is to make the person more accurately aware of all his/her characteristics and be more open to experience.

A few more characteristics of the self deserve notice. As mentioned, the self is entirely conscious and as such is measurable for purposes of research or therapy. The self does not "do" anything; the self does not control the person's behavior. The self symbolizes the person's own experience of the environment; the perception of the self follows the general laws of perception discussed earlier. In line with the need for organization also previously discussed, the self-concept is an organized and consistent whole, a pattern of related perceptions. The self-concept may change somewhat as new experiences are added, but will retain the general organization.

Much research has supported the notion of congruency of choice, i.e., product choice, with the person's perceptions of themselves. The example of the relationship between car choice and self-image was given previously. The person continues to seek consistency in experience. This will be dealt with more fully when attitude consistency is considered. Although the percentage of variance in behavior explained in any study using personality theory is not high, the percentages are significant. This is not surprising, considering the other influences which also operate in a decision-making situation. In any case, the person's attitudes and preferences toward various products or other objects appear to be unquestionably affected by the person's personality characteristics, whether explicitly as in Cattell's theory or implicitly as in other theories.

APPLICATION OF THEORIES

Cattell's Theory and the Growth of Consumer Credit
by David Sills

Cattell's theory of personality may be applied to analyze differences among people in the age of credit. He states that a person's behavior is a function of personality traits and the situation a person finds himself or herself in. Cattell has developed three components which make up personality traits. The first is ergs; these are inherited traits. The second component of personality traits is sentiment, which is learned. The third is attitude. This concept of attitude is developed by interaction of ergs and sentiment.

Ergs, traits which are largely inherited, are less likely to affect the use of credit by an individual than would sentiment or the situation one finds oneself in. However, in general, if one's parents are conservative by nature and traits relating to this are passed on to their children, this may affect the way that child will use credit in the future.

Cattell's second component (sentiment) is largely learned through one's social environment. This particular environment in which an individual develops his/her sentiments could greatly affect the extent and manner in which credit is used by an individual. Since the use of credit cards is primarily a middle-class phenomenon today (Anon. 1968), a person born and raised in this class will be more likely to view a credit card as a symbol of security than a person raised in an upper income environment. Whereas the middle-class person would use the credit card for installment purchases as well as convenience, the upper-class person is more prone to use a credit card for convenience and a temporary replacement for cash (Mathews and Slocum 1969).

The third component of personality traits, attitudes, are developed by ergs or sentiments, or the interaction of both. It is obvious that a person's attitudes toward credit will have a marked influence over a person's use of credit. This idea is more fully developed later in this paper when Katz's theories of attitude change are analyzed with respect to the use of credit.

The other factor which influences a person's behavior according to Cattell is the situation one finds oneself in. Although Cattell does not stress this factor when analyzing consumer behavior in general, this factor is very important when it is related to the use of credit cards. For example, if a family were to go to dinner and upon receiving the bill discover they have no cash on hand, they would more than likely use a credit card to pay the bill.

Attitudes towards credit are subject to change. This point becomes obvious if one compares attitudes towards credit in America in the early 1900s to those of present day attitudes in America. The early American would probably say that a consumer who uses credit to secure luxury goods is foolish. On the other hand, a person in America today would probably think that this is merely a way of living up to the standards achievable today.

The functional approach Katz (1960) has towards attitude and attitude change seems to analyze this change in attitude toward credit most clearly. Katz describes four factors which affect attitude change. First, if the good (in this case credit) no longer provides the same satisfaction as before, the individual's attitude towards credit will change. This could occur if the finance charges were increased on the individual's credit card. In this situation the individual's desire to use credit would almost certainly go down.

Katz's second point in this theory has to do with ego defense. This states that a person will not do something that is contrary to his/her self-concept. Thus, the early American would not use credit while the present-day American would. No one likes to think he or she is stupid; the idea of ego does not allow this. Because of this, the early American would not use credit since its use would have been contrary to his/her self-concept.

Value expressive is Katz's third idea. This states that an individual's values, beliefs and self-image will affect his/her behavior. If a person is basically conservative, it is unlikely that he/she will use credit to the extent a more adventurous person might, as the use of credit relies upon speculation on future earnings as its mainstay.

Finally, with regard to Katz's theory vis-a-vis knowledge and its impact on attitude, one sees that as the level of knowledge in economic theory increased from the early 1900s to the present in America, certain attitudinal changes were inevitable. The impact of the great Depression on these attitudes was most significant. When the idea of deficit spending was introduced, for example, a marked change of attitudes toward credit occurred.

The resources used in this paper were mainly from the late 1960s when our gross national product (GNP) was about $800 billion. Presently our gross national product is $1 trillion plus. The amount of debt our society runs on is massive. This makes it all the more important that the Federal Reserve authorities maintain a constant watch on the money supply to ensure that interest rates do not fluctuate too erratically. Any upward fluctuations in interest rates are transmitted and amplified through the society. This could cause considerable consumer suffering.

Consumers have an equally important role in the stability of the economy. They must use credit with responsibility. If consumers as a group were to overextend themselves financially and be unable to honor their debts, grave repercussions would result. Entire financial institutions could be wiped out. Thus, if we are to continue to reap the advantages of a credit-oriented society and the increased consumption that goes with it, both the government and consumers as a group must act responsibly in the future.

Horney's Theory and the Choice of Clothing
by Linda Wildensteiner

People's choice of clothing is derived from several motives. Decoration, aesthetic expression and enhancement of the attractiveness of the body have long been primary motives for dress, especially among primitive peoples. Although comfort and protection from heat and cold, insects, thorny underbrush and stony terrain are important considerations, according to Latzke and Hostetter (1968) these are secondary motives. A person may purchase a leather jacket for motorcycling, ostensibly for protection in case of a fall, but fashion and attractiveness are the decision criteria.

Fashion is the most commanding force in a person's choice of dress. As fashion changes, garments become socially obsolete. Conformity tends to become so important that all other needs and values are overlooked. This is especially true during the teenage years when teenagers will sacrifice comfort, economy, health and even becomingness in order to obtain social acceptance (Troelstrup 1970). If mini-skirts were "in," a young woman would buy one just for the approval of the group even if it was not flattering to her (Latzke and Hostetter 1968). Clothes also play a major role in attracting the opposite sex, and the definition of alluring clothing is shaped by fashion. In some years, loose-fitting clothes are thought to be sexy because of the element of intrigue. In other years, tight-fitting clothes are favored because they outline the figure.

Conformity also operates through societal definitions of modesty and through the association of clothing with social prestige. The definition of modesty seems to fluctuate with the times and depends on the customs of each culture, so a motive of modesty for wearing clothing is actually one of conformity. Clothing as a means of conformity has also served as a ticket for admission into different social groups. The fur coat is seen as a sign of social prestige, primarily because it is expensive (Dichter 1964). In the 1960s, blue denim became the dress code of the counterculture. The counterculture used its clothing as a weapon for defiance of authority, or as a symbol of revolt and nonconformity.

In accordance with the expressive aspect of clothing, people dress in such a way as to project their own personalities (Latzke and Hostetter 1968). Politicians dress to match the political personality they are trying to portray during a campaign. Two illustrations of this are George McGovern and Jimmy Carter. McGovern ran as the liberal, social welfare oriented candidate against the more conservative, business oriented Nixon. One look at McGovern's campaign literature instantly gave one that impression. McGovern wore long sideburns, flared pants and colorful shirt and tie combinations before they were fully accepted for business wear. Carter, running as a liberal-minded populist, was many times clad in plaid shirts and corduroy pants during his campaign in order to project a "back-home" image.

Most people also tend to buy those clothes which fit them in a psychological sense (Dichter 1964). The above considerations of self-expression and conformity to fashion will be more important to some individuals than to others and different individuals will react differently with respect to them, depending on the type of personality an individual has. This is the essence behind Cohen's study, which is based on Karen Horney's Interpersonal Model, a neoFreudian approach.

Horney felt that childhood insecurities resulting from parent-child relationships create anxieties which the person learns to cope with, and the way in which an individual copes with those anxieties makes up his/her personality (Kassarjian and Robertson 1973). Horney placed people into three groups depending on their primary mode of response to others: (1) compliant—those who move toward others, (2) aggressive—those who move against people, and (3) detached—those who move away from people.

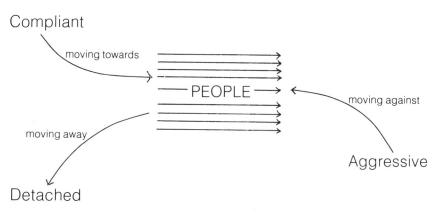

The orientation a person selects depends upon which one proves the most successful for him/her. He/she will then adopt those values consistent with his/her view of others. However, people don't always stick with one orientation; it may change with the situation (Holloway *et al.* 1971).

The predominant strategy, which this author will be concerned with, is a function of (1) previous reinforcement (based on present attitudes) and (2) the perceived relevance of the type of behavior in a situation. The relevance of the three orientations described has yet to be empirically determined, but some consumer decisions, such as buying clothes, may be strongly motivated by interpersonal response traits. The purchase of a particular garment or style of dress not only reveals the desired interpersonal orientation to other people, but it reinforces and is consistent with the values associated with the individual's self-concept (Holloway *et al.* 1971).

Cohen's study, which covered a wide range of products including men's dress shirts, found that differences in product use and brand choice were attributed to differences in interpersonal orientations (Robertson 1970). Based on advertisements for "Van Heusen" shirts, it was predicted that more aggressive men would be attracted to that brand. The results confirmed this—high aggressive men did prefer "Van Heusen" shirts to other shirts to a significantly greater extent than low aggressive men. The Cohen study also concluded that a slightly higher percentage of detached people rather than compliant or aggressive people did not know what brand they used most often. In general, it expected that detached individuals are less aware of or concerned with brand names as indicators of "social status" than compliant or aggressive individuals (Holloway *et al.* 1971).

Analogous to the men's "Van Heusen" shirts would be women's "Bloomingdale" dresses. A "Bloomingdale" dress is the very expensive, fashionable, prestigious, one-of-a-kind garment which the more aggressive woman would have to have. The "Bloomingdale" shopper would be noticed and admired, or thought of as a snob because her dress would give the effect of superiority and status. As the compliant woman is more humble and less egotistical, she would not have much desire for a "Bloomingdale" outfit unless she felt it would help her to be part of a group. The detached woman would have no need for such expensive clothing and probably would have been turned off by any ads she might have heard or seen as to why a "Bloomingdale" outfit is a must for any woman's wardrobe.

Horney's model, then, suggests that people buy clothing to fit their type. The aggressive, outgoing woman would be attracted to bright colors, splashy prints and the most unique clothes. She would be among the first wearing the new fashions and would be among those to set the trend in style. The detached woman would find subdued colors and modest patterns more appropriate and would not be concerned with fashion; she would wear clothes to suit her own tastes and no one else's (Latzke and Hostetter 1968). The compliant woman would join the bandwagon—purchase the types of clothes her peers and those in her social group were wearing.

The art elements—line, form, color and texture—are the building blocks used in creating any design, including clothes designing. The importance attached to any one of these elements stems partly from a physical law and partly from its emotional connotation derived from the individual's previous experience with that element. For example, an aggressive woman may have discovered that by wearing a "Mondrian-inspired" shift, with its strong oppositional lines of bold colors crisscrossing in a windowpane effect, she possessed a feeling of dignity and strength. It was the direction, character and color of the line that conveyed to her the impression of strength and power which served to reinforce her self-orientation of being aggressive (Latzke and Hostetter 1968). This same impression would probably arouse distaste in the detached-oriented woman as she would prefer clothes of a subdued nature and tone but with a marked color sense. The compliant woman would not find the "Mondrian-inspired" shift too appealing as she would choose clothing that stresses harmony and fitness of colors (Anspach 1967). Texture is the element of design that refers to the appearance and feel of the surface of a material. It also inspires some degree of emotional response so that textures can be selected to reflect an individual's self-concept. For example, fabrics that project the image of boldness, self-confidence and sophistication for the aggressive-oriented woman are tweedy tweeds, leathers, velour and wide-wale corduroy (Kefgen and Touchie-Specht 1971).

In conclusion, Horney's model and Cohen's study of it indicate that different interpersonal orientations result in compliant, aggressive and detached people buying different styles of clothing. As the person's self-concept or orientation is of value and of central importance, he/she will direct his/her behavior, in this case his/her purchase of clothes, to maintain and enhance his/her self-image (McNeal 1969).

Self Theory and the Effects of Sexist Advertising
by Karen Selsor

Society today is in a state of flux. The surfacing of the Women's Liberation Movement is but one social phenomenon to which this societal change may be attributed. Feminism, while perhaps not embraced ideologically by the majority of women in America, has nevertheless had a profound effect on all spheres of society. More than twice as many women have had some college training as had 20 years ago and significantly more women are earning professional degrees. The number of working women increased 35% during the 1964–1974 period. Women are now being accepted in jobs formerly considered to be exclusively male (Anon. 1975A). There are thus many indicators that the dichotomization of the sexes is narrowing and that women's social and work roles are expanding at a very rapid rate. Concomitantly, women's attitudes, values and perceptions of themselves would seem to be undergoing transformations as well. Yet, in the area of consumer behavior, according to Courtney and Whipple (1974), advertisers are lagging far behind role changes in their portrayal of women.

Feminists are of course particularly sensitized to sexism in advertising; their reactions tend toward polemics. Nevertheless, the humiliating images of women in advertising may be working toward raising even *non*feminist consciousness. A National Advertising Review Board panel recently examined the basis for complaints about advertising that portrays women or is directed to them. Of the consumers they interviewed:

"...Some were outspoken feminists, some were at the other end of the spectrum. The panel found that, while there was considerable difference in their rhetoric, frequently there were only small differences in their *attitudes* toward advertising that involved women...Even women who don't consider themselves part of an 'oppressed class' may accept and even espouse criticism of advertising...Thus the criticism of advertising considered demeaning to women may fall on fertile ground and spread...It would appear, therefore, that the more vocal critics of advertising as 'sexist' are younger, better educated, more articulate women who often are opinion leaders. On the average, they have more discretionary income. As their numbers increase...their challenge to advertising will probably become greater, unless constructive action is taken" (Anon. 1975A).

Based on the assumption that women are changing their perceptions, attitudes and values as their roles within the home and outside the home expand, this paper will discuss the evidence that advertising is trailing far behind the role changes of women, the effects that traditional (sexist) advertising might have on a woman's buying behavior (perception and self theory will be incorporated into the discussion here) and predictions and recommendations emphasizing how advertisers must adopt new strategies and methods if their products are going to continue to do well.

Images of Women In Advertising—Are Marketers Keeping Up?—A review of the literature provides evidence that advertisers are indeed lagging far behind role changes in their portrayal of women. Most of the censure has in fact originated from individuals (men and women) within the advertising industry. Their critiques range from purely impressionistic data to field surveys and empirical laboratory studies. Following is a sampling of the research in the area of the portrayal of women in advertising. Only recent articles were considered for inclusion and are arranged chronologically.[1]

In the July 22, 1974 issue of *Advertising Age*, a survey (sample size unreported) by the Behavior Research Institute is reviewed. The findings of the survey were, in sum, that advertisers "don't understand yet how the female consumer lives or learns. Women do not buy because of some vague inner impulse or some mysterious subconscious urge...Too many marketers still picture the female consumer as fudging the checking account and lying about her age" (Baltera 1974).

The Journal of Advertising Research in August 1974 featured an article concerning women in magazine advertisements. Haberman and Sexton (1974) evaluated 1827 ads for tobacco, non-alcoholic beverages, automobiles, home appliances, office equipment and airline travel (as products used equally by both sexes) in five nationally circulated magazines (*Good Housekeeping, Look, Newsweek, Sports Illustrated* and *TV Guide*). Their over-

---

[1]This paper was written in the fall of 1976.

all results revealed that images of women reflected in magazine advertisements are quite narrow, with only 16% depicting women in nontraditional situations and with 30% of the cigarette, beverage, auto and airline ads portraying women as alluring "sex symbols."

In *The Journal of Communication*, September 1974, Courtney and Whipple provide analyses from four separate studies which focused on the depiction of women in television commercials. Their results provide cogent evidence that women are not portrayed as autonomous, independent human beings but are primarily sex-typed. For example, 87% to 89% of both daytime and nightime commercials use male voiceovers, regardless of type of product or sex of the model in the commercial. Men, as traditional authority figures, are thus evidently seen by advertisers as being more effective in the actual verbal selling of their products. An equal number of men and women are used as product representatives (models) during daytime television commercials, but men are significantly more likely to be shown as product representatives at night (during prime time television). But 74% of all ads using women as models are for bathroom and kitchen products. They conclude that: "Women's roles continue to change and expand at a faster rate than the advertiser's response during that time period. Advertisers are lagging far behind role changes in their protrayal of women. In that sense, television commercials are not getting better but may be getting worse" (Courtney and Whipple 1974).

Wortsel and Frisbie present an empirical study of women's role portrayal preferences in advertisements in the October 1974 issue of the *Journal of Marketing*. This study asked two questions: what role portrayals are most likely to make the product being advertised appear most desirable to women, and, do women who believe most strongly in the tenets of the women's liberation movement also tend most strongly to perceive a product as more desirable when the women in the advertisement is portrayed in a working role? The 100 subjects in their experiment were asked to "design" their own advertisements by matching 21 products (small appliances, large appliances, women's grooming products, household products, women's personal products, foods, and men's grooming and personal products) with one of five background environments provided to them in a portfolio of photographs (in which women were depicted either in "neutral," "family," "career," "sex object," or "fashion object" roles). After the subject "designed" her ads and the product-picture matches were recorded, each was given a pencil-and-paper measure of her attitudes towards the women's liberation movement. The major conclusion reached by these investigators was that: "If the product is one that is normally used in a household environment, then women (both liberationists and nonliberationists) prefer to see it in this type of setting ...If the product is one that women use personally, which somehow enhances their concept of themselves as women, then nontraditional roles are preferred" (Wortzel and Frisbie 1974).

The National Advertising Review Board in a special report analyzed a broad sampling of current advertising portraying or directed to women, reviewed current literature on the subject and interviewed many consumers, both profeminists and antifeminists. In general, the panel found that advertising has been slow to reflect the occupational changes experienced by women during the past 20 years, that women are most often portrayed as housewives and sex objects, and that "it is the unanimous conclusion of the panel that any attempt to improve the situation will accomplish two important goals. First, it will provide a greater measure of fair treatment for women. Second, it will be an intelligent marketing decision (Anon. 1975A).

However, the attitudes of advertisers are slow to change despite the rather extensive report of the NARB. The June 16, 1975 issue of *Advertising Age* carries an article entitled "Ads ignore real women, use stereotypes"; even specific trade magazines such as *Drug and Cosmetic Industries* chide advertisers for their limited views of women (Anon. 1975B). The writer's personal observations[2] also support these allegations; the "consciousness" of advertisers seems to be immutable.

In sum, it appears that marketers are not fully cognizant of certain basic principles of psychological theory as applied to consumer behavior. Let us now examine these principles in order to specify how today's "enlightened" woman as a consumer might react to continued traditional (sexist) ads and

---

[2] The examples are legion, but largely subjective. Thus they are left out of this discussion so as not to introduce the personal biases of the writer.

products, and to determine which products are most apt to be affected unless advertising strategies are modified. In a final section, specific recommendations will be made to advertisers in their efforts to reach the widest market without alienating a large portion of that market.

Female Consumer Behavior and Sexism in Advertising: Perception and Self-concept Theories.—Perception is the process by which meaning and structure are attached to sensory inputs. The perception of a product depends on the physical and symbolic attributes of the product (the nature of the product, its brand image, package design and advertisement) as well as on the cognitive set (personality, mood, need-value system, self-concept) of the consumer to whom the product is being presented. According to Horowitz and Kaye (1975), how an individual consumer perceives a product depends on how well it agrees with his/her personal cognitve world. The importance of brand images in the perception of products has been established from several studies (see Allison and Uhl (1968) and Makens (1965)); in addition, the symbolic imagery presented in advertising and associated with the product (through depiction of the product representative, colors used, message content, etc.) has been found to be influential in determining how the individual will perceive the product. Say Horowitz and Kaye (1975):

"The product does not exist in a vacuum, but...in various symbolic forms in the cognitive world of the consumer. An advertiser must be aware of the possible symbolization that a product may acquire, of the form of symbolization most probable in a market segment, and of the methods used to promote the product as a particular symbol."

In order to theoretically link the symbolic attributes of a product to the cognitive set of the consumer, Grubb and Grathwohl (1967) have proposed an approach relating the psychological construct of self-concept to the symbolic image of the product (since self-concept has more specific operational referents than does personality, and thus would lend itself more reliably to empirical measurement). If the symbolic image of the product as presented in its advertisements reinforces the person's self-concept or allows him/her to identify with some positively valued reference group, then the perception of the product will be enhanced. Thus, Grubb and Grathwohl predict that only those products with images that are acceptable to or consistent with the self-image will be considered by the consumer.[3] For example, Dolich investigated relationships between self-concept and product images, using the semantic differential to measure both, and he found that the preferred brands were evaluated as significantly more congruent with self-concept than the non-preferred brands (Horowitz and Kaye 1975).

The implications of the theories of perception and of the self are clear: if women are currently expanding their self-concepts to encompass more autonomous and less sex-typed behavioral roles, then advertisers must recognize this. They must reduce the psychological distance between the self and product image by using themes, slogans and product representatives that are descriptive of the self-image of the intended consumer. One example of this is a National Life Insurance of Vermont advertisement which shows a woman sitting behind a microscope. "She's working to make your life better," says the caption. "She's a biochemist...The same motivation drives our agents in serving your life insurance needs" (Komisar 1971).

The actual physical attributes of the product (the nature of the product) may also not be congruent with the individual's self-concept. This might have special significance and application to the cosmetic and clothing industries. Young women and modern feminists are more and more rejecting the "cult of beauty" that has pervaded our society during the last few decades. Here the woman's self-concept is inconsistent with the product itself, not just with the way it is advertised (its symbolic imagery). With

---

[3] This is derived from Carl Rogers' self theory and uses his Q-sort technique as an operational measure of self-concept. According to Rogers, the self consists of those values, attitudes, emotions and strivings that an individual recognizes as his/her own, as part of the "I" and "me." The overriding motivational need of the person is the actualizing tendency, which represents "the inherent tendency of the organism to develop all its capacities in ways which serve to maintain or enhance the person." The actualizing tendency serves as the criterion against which all of a person's life experiences are evaluated. Any experiences which are inconsistent with the self-concept (which in general also tend to weaken the actualizing tendency) are not symbolized in awareness. Thus behaviors emitted by an individual are those which are congruent with the value-belief system that he/she assumes represents him/herself (DiCaprio 1974).

some ingenuity, however, it is conceivable that marketers could bring these individuals back into the cosmetic market through changing the product image from one that is blatantly glamorous and connected to "trapping a man" to one that focuses more on the intrinsic and aesthetic rewards of looking one's best.

Let us now consider ways in which advertisers can use self theory in order to avoid alienating the woman who is changing her self-perceptions and who will, it may be predicted, change her buying behavior unless this is taken into account.

Intelligent Advertising for Intelligent Consumers—Application of Principles.—"When all the evidence is summed up, it would appear that it is not just a lack of manners or a lack of social responsibility, but actually a counter-productive business practice to try to sell a product to someone who feels insulted by the product's advertising" (Anon. 1975A).

And, from Amelia Bassin in the October 1975 issue of *Drug and Cosmetic Industries*, a challenge to the beauty business: "The next step, I hope, is for someone to jump right in that market and really grab that liberated woman. There are all kinds of ways to do it—maybe not our usual sweet-nothing double talk, but some straight talking real talk...You needn't embrace the women's lib movement; just don't stab it" (Bassin 1975).

Here then are some specific recommendations, based on theories presented in this paper, that might be offered to advertisers.

From self theory and perception, it might be recommended that the themes, slogans and product representatives used in advertisements be more descriptive of today's modern woman, and that old stereotypes be left behind. More emphasis should be directed to the woman in her "work" role, and when the role of homemaker is portrayed, it should not be depicted in a grotesque or stereotyped manner. In sum, efforts should be made to reach the woman as thinker, rather than the woman as consumer.

The principles discussed in this paper would seem especially applicable to development of brand loyalty and the adoption of new products. In addition, certain industries and businesses would seem to be most affected (such as the cosmetics and clothing industries, as already mentioned, and the entertainment, travel, automobile and convenience foods industries, since working women's incomes are spent in these areas). Much more research certainly needs to be undertaken, but one thing seems clear: advertisers who take the modern woman into account are likely to rate higher with *all* women.

REFERENCES

ALLISON, R. and UHL, K. 1968. Influence of beer brand identification on taste perceptions. J. Marktg. Res. *5*, 35-40.

ANON. 1968. Bank Credit-card and Check-credit Plans. Publications Services, Division of Administrative Service, U.S. Board of Governors of the Federal Reserve System, Washington, D.C.

ANON. 1975A. Advertising portraying or directed to women. Adver. Age *46*, 72-74.

ANON. 1975B. Ads ignore real women, use stereotypes. Drug Cosmetic Indus. *10*, 34.

ANSPACH, K. 1967. The Why of Fashion. Iowa State Univ. Press, Ames.

BALTERA, L. 1974. The working woman's come a long way, but can advertisers find her? Adver. Age *45*, 2.

BANDURA, A. 1965. Influence of models' reinforcement contingencies on the acquisition of imitative responses, J. Personality Soc. Psychol. *1*, 589-595

BANDURA, A. 1969A. Principles of Behavior Modification. Holt, Rinehart, and Winston, New York.

BANDURA, A. 1969B. Social-learning theory of identification processes. *In* Handbook of Socialization Theory and Research. (D.A. Goslin, Editor.) Rand McNally, Chicago.

BANDURA, A. 1971. Analysis of modeling processes. *In* Psychological Modeling. (A. Bandura, Editor.) Aldine-Atherton, Chicago.

BANDURA, A. and MISCHEL, W. 1965. Modification of self-imposed delay of reward through exposure to live and symbolic models. J. Personality Soc. Psychol. *2*, 698-705

BANDURA, A. and WALTERS, R. H. 1963. Social Learning and Personality Development. Holt, Rinehart and Winston, New York.

BASSIN, A. 1975. Advertising to women: Limited. Drug and Cosmetic Indus. *10*, 34.

CATTELL, R. 1957. Personality and Motivation: Structure and Measurement. World Book Company, New York.

CATTELL, R. 1959. Personality theory growing from multivariate quantitative research. *In* Psychology: A Study of Science. Vol. 3. (Sigmund Koch, Editor.) McGraw-Hill, New York.

CATTELL, R. 1965. The Scientific Analysis of Personality. Aldine Publishing Company, Chicago.

COHEN, J. 1967. An interpersonal orientation to the study of consumer behavior. J. Market. Res. *4*, 270-278.

COURTNEY, A. E. and WHIPPLE, T. W. 1974. Women in television commercials. J. Comm. *24*, 35.

DICAPRIO, N. S. 1974. Personality Theories: Guides to Living. W. B. Saunders Co., Philadelphia.

DICHTER, E. 1964. Handbook of Consumer Motivations. McGraw-Hill Book Co., Boston.

DOLLARD, J. and MILLER, N. 1950. Personality and Psychotherapy, McGraw-Hill, New York.

EYSENCK, H. 1953. The Structure of Human Personality. Mathuean, London.

GRUBB, E. L. and GRATHWOHL, H. L. 1967. Consumer self-concept, symbolism and market behavior: A theoretical approach. J. Market. *31* (10) 22-27.

HABERMAN, P. and SEXTON, D. E. 1974. Women in magazine advertisement. J. Adver. Res. *14*, 41-46.

HOLLOWAY, MITTELSTAEDT and VENKATESAN. 1971. Consumer Behavior. Houghton Mifflin Co., Boston.

HORNEY, K. 1945. Our Inner Conflicts. Norton, New York.

HOROWITZ, I. A. and KAYE, R. S. 1975. Perceptions and advertising. J. Adver. Res. *15*, 15-21.

KASSARJIAN and ROBERTSON. 1973. Perspectives in Consumer Behavior. Scott, Foresman and Co., Illinois.

KATZ, D. 1960. The functional approach to the study of attitudes. Public Opinion Quart. *24*, 163-204.

KEFGEN and TOUCHIE-SPECHT. 1971. Individuality in Clothing Selection and Personal Appearance. McMillian Co., N.Y.

KOMISAR, L. 1971. The image of women in advertising. *In* Woman in Sexist Society. (Gornic and Moran, Editors) Basic Books, New York.

LATZKE and HOSTETTER. 1968. The Wide World of Clothing. Ronald Press Co., New York.

MAKENS, J. 1965. Effect of brand preference upon consumers' perceived taste of turkey meat. J. Appl. Psychol. *49* (4) 261-263.

MATHEWS, H. and SLOCUM, J. 1969. Social class and commercial bank credit card usage. J. Market. *33*, 71-78.

MCNEAL, J. U. 1969. Dimensions of Consumer Behavior. Meredith Corp., New York.

PERVIN, L. 1975. Personality: Theory, Assessment and Research. John Wiley and Sons, New York.

ROBERTSON, T. S. 1970. Consumer Behavior. Scott, Foresman and Co., Illinois.

ROBINSON, L. 1970. Marijuana Use in High School Girls: A Psycho-social Case Study. Masters thesis. University of Maryland, College Park.

ROGERS, C. 1959. A theory of therapy, personality and interpersonal relationships as developed in the client-centered framework. *In* Psychology: A Study of a Science. Vol. 3. (Sigmund Koch, Editor.) McGraw-Hill, New York.

TROELSTRUP, A. W. 1970. The Consumer in American Society. McGraw-Hill Book Co., New York.

WORTZEL, L. and FRISBIE, J. 1974. Women's role portrayal preferences in advertisements: an empirical study. J. Market. *38*, 41-46.

6

Factors Affecting Attitudes: Social Influences

Rogers views the self as formed largely through internal mechanisms, although he does indicate that the "conditions of worth" are learned. Other theorists give more emphasis to the social factors shaping a person's self-concept, personality, preferences and choices. This characterization especially holds for some theorists, such as Mead and Cooley, who deal with symbolic interaction.

SYMBOLIC INTERACTION

Symbolic interaction focuses on the meaning connoted by gestures. Gestures are symbolic; humans respond to one another on the basis of their interpretations of other's gestures. A person who interprets a pat on the shoulder as an indication of concern will react differently than if he/she interprets it as an act of aggression. The basis for human society then becomes the sharing of meanings attached to gestures.

Individuals can also respond to their own gestures. The person making the gesture has an image of the intended meaning, just as does the person perceiving the gesture. The actor intends for the perceiver to respond in a certain way and while acting imagines the person's response. This rests upon the shared meaning of the gesture. The act of imagining the perceiver's response requires role-taking; the actor must identify with the perceiver and put him/herself in the perceiver's place.

The concept of self emerges here in that the individual may react to him/herself as well as to others, such as in self-praise, self-blame and self-punishment. Thus, the person can be the object of his/her own behavior. The self under this theory is social in nature; it is formed through the reactions of other people. Charles Horton Cooley (1930) terms this the "looking-glass self." The mechanism by which the self develops is role-taking; the person can view him/herself as an object by taking the role of another person. Language is vitally important in the development of the self in that this is the way the person learns the meanings of the gestures of others including those toward him or her.

Mead (Meltzer 1964) proposed two phases of the self, the *I* and the *Me*. The *I* is the individual's spontaneous impulse to act. The *Me* represents the set of meanings common to the society in which the individual is acting. The *I* initiates the act and the *Me* regulates the act.

The self has considerable implications for behavior:

(1) "The possession of a self makes of the individual a society in miniature. That is, he may engage in interaction with himself just as two or more different individuals might. In the course of this interaction he can come to view himself in a new way, thereby bringing about changes in himself.

(2) "The ability to act toward oneself makes possible an inner experience which need not reach overt expression. That is, the individual, by virtue of having a self, is thereby endowed with the possibility of having a mental life: He can make indications to himself—which constitutes *mind*.

(3) "The individual with a self is thereby enabled to direct and control his behavior. Instead of being subject to all impulses and stimuli directly playing upon him, the individual can check, guide and organize his behavior. He is, then, *not* a mere passive agent" (Meltzer 1964).

Kinch (1963) has proposed a formalized theory of the self-concept, which he defines as the organization of qualities (attributes and roles) that the individual attributes to him/herself. In general, the basic idea of his theory is that the individual's conception of him/herself emerges from social interaction and in turn guides or influences the behavior of that individual.

There are four basic concepts in this theory:

(1) the individual's self-concept (S);
(2) the individual's perception of the responses of others toward him or her, or at least which he/she perceives as directed toward him or her (P);
(3) the actual responses of others toward the individual (A); and
(4) the individual's behavior (B).

Three postulates are stated:

(1) the individual's self-concept is based on his/her perception of the way others are responding to him or her (P→S),
(2) the individual's self-concept serves to direct his/her behavior (S→B), and
(3) the individual's perception of the responses of others toward him/her reflects the actual responses of others toward him or her (A→P).

By use of deductive logic, more propositions can be derived such as:

(4) the way the individual perceives the responses of others toward him/her will influence his/her behavior (P→B, from statements 1 and 2),
(5) the actual responses of others to the individual will determine the way he/she sees him/herself (his/her self-concept) (A→S, from statements 1 and 3), and
(6) the actual responses of others toward the individual will

affect the behavior of the individual (A→B, from either statements 2 and 5 or 3 and 4).

A chain therefore develops, of A→P→S→B. The actual behavior of others affects the indivdual's perception of that behavior, which then affects the individual's self-concept and, in turn, the individual's behavior. But since this individual is also an "other" person to these "others" referred to above, the individual's actual behavior toward them affects their self-concepts and subsequently their own behavior. This includes their behavior toward this individual. Therefore, a new postulate can be added:

(7) The behavior that the individual manifests influences the actual responses of others toward that individual (B→A).

The chain of influence now becomes a circle: A→P→S→B→A. One may then derive a whole new set of propositions.

The extent to which the postulates hold vary with circumstances. For example, consider the relationship of the person's perception of the responses of others to their actual responses. The phenomenon of selective perception has been discussed previously. The person's perception may or may not concur with what the other persons intended by their symbolic gestures. Several factors could influence the convergence of these symbolic interpretations. The accuracy of postulate 3 appears to vary with (1) the individual's familiarity with the others, (2) his/her familiarity with the situation, (3) the social visibility of the situation, (4) the individual's past experience in interpersonal situations, and (5) other factors which relate to all types of perception, such as conditions of body, immediate past, etc. (Kinch 1963).

The interactionists, while continuing to focus on the individual, place the individual from the beginning in a social context. Society shapes the kind of person the individual becomes and as such influences his/her values, attitudes and preferences and in turn his/her behavior. Other research has been concerned with the individual in a group context, but has dealt directly with group influence on the individual's attitudes and behavior.

THE NATURE OF GROUPS

Cattell's theory of individual personality has been considered previously. Cattell and Stice (1960) have extended this theory to deal with relations of individuals to individuals, between groups and individuals, and groups to groups. The method of analysis is the same; Cattell applies to group behavior the same factor analytic methods he uses for individuals in an attempt to discover the functional dimensions of behavior.

He uses several basic theoretical concepts and assumptions as follows:

(1) A group is distinguished from a mere aggregate by the fact that each individual contributes to the satisfaction of all. The group is an instrument for satisfying individual needs. A group can be defined only secondarily by interaction; the primary unity is the dynamic one.

(2) A full description of any group requires attention to the three following aspects.

   (a) *Population* or personnel profile, i.e., the mean and variation of the members of the group on all parameters of individuals, e.g., intelligence, personality, attitudes, beliefs, customs.

   (b) The *structure* of the group, which defines the roles and relationships, exists in principle independently of the personnel.

   (c) The *syntality*, which is defined analogously to the personality of the individual, deals with the behavior of the group in its acts as a unified body. It is that which permits prediction of the behavior of the group, as a group, in a defined stimulus situation.

(3) The total synergy of a group is the total energy which goes into its operations. This will be a function of the number of people in the group and the amount of satisfaction which they get out of it. This synergy depends on individual attitudes, and may itself be factor analyzed to discover its dimensions. The sources of synergy include several major

kinds of satisfaction for the members. These include the following.

(a) *Leadership synergy*, the extent to which the leader is able to show that the group is capable of satisfying members' needs, or to open up new needs that the group can satisfy. A leader, under Cattell's theory, is a problem solver for the group and is defined objectively in terms of effect on group syntality (in contrast to a leader defined by group structure).

(b) Immediate group *sociability synergy*, the satisfaction in belonging to a group which arises largely from gregarious satisfactions.

(c) *Status synergy*, the satisfactions which persons get from self-assertiveness, appreciation of others, etc., in the various roles and offices.

(d) *Personal gain synergy*, such satisfactions as salary and other contributions to generalized ergic needs of individuals as individuals.

(4) The syntality, structure and personnel profile of groups should be related in such a way that, with ideal knowledge of social psychological laws, and of the particular personalities and group roles, it would be possible to deduce syntality from structure and personnel. This strongly resembles his view concerning the predictability of individual behavior.

Upon empirical investigation, Cattell did find characteristics relating to population, structure and syntality. The syntality characteristics, the least stable among the three, improved as the group became older. In general, he concluded that the origins of the group dimensions must be traced to personality differences in the populations, to environmental causes such as choice of leader, and to certain accidental differences due to fatigue, hunger, etc., which then take on more than their original importance in their influence on group development.

The personality of the leader can account for major group differences. The personalities of the selected leaders themselves differ significantly from the personalities of followers. In particular, leaders were less susceptible to threats, more confident and less timid, and had stronger moral character and control. Moral character is necessary for stability and good judgment in dealing with difficulties. A person given to anxiety generally cannot tolerate well the responsibilities and aggression from followers. A more outgoing personality can better communicate feelings and ideas.

Another indication from the research was that as the group is longer in existence, population characteristics become overshadowed by group structure in importance in determining syntality characteristics. Also, the personality characteristics of individuals significantly affect the way in which they interact with others. For example, an easy-going, trustful, generous person gives more socioemotional support than ideas on how to solve a given problem, and a submissive person participates less than others.

Cattell concluded that if one could obtain factor patterns with as great consistency as appeared in his experimental study, in just formed and short lived groups which did not contain great sources of difference, one could be even more confident in factoring behavior of longer established, ongoing groups. Thus, he extended his theory of the personality of the individual to apply to the personality of the group.

A somewhat more conventional way of looking at groups describes them in terms of their structure and function. The interaction of people over time constitutes a major difference between a group and a collection of people who happen to be in the same location at the same time. For example, on many cross-country bus trips the passengers simply get on, sit down, and read a book or sleep until they get off. They do not form any kind of a group. If they begin talking and interacting with the other passengers, either through their own desire or initiated by some unusual circumstance, they then become a group.

The structure of a group involves these interaction patterns. The members take on roles in dealing with each other; that is, a person in a particular position in a group is expected to act in a certain way. If all act in accordance with expectations, the group can perform its functions smoothly because few misunderstandings arise.

Some roles carry more prestige than do others; as such, a status hierarchy within the group develops. Often, the status of a role correlates with the centrality of its position within the group's communication network. For example, consider groups with communication patterns like these:

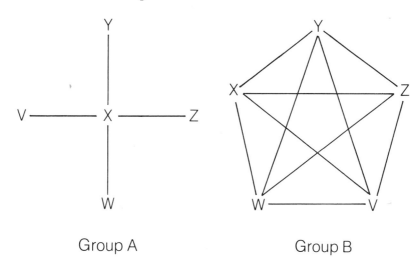

Group A   Group B

In Group A, all communication goes through person X. The other members have no contact with each other. X thus occupies a very central position. If X suddenly vanishes, group functioning will cease, at least until someone takes over X's position or a new communication pattern develops. If V, W, Y or Z vanishes, group functioning proceeds with comparatively little disruption. Since X's position has such importance, it probably will carry with it a high status. In Group B, everyone communicates with everyone else. No one has a more central position than anyone else. Therefore, one would expect all roles to be comparatively equal in status, since all are equally important at least on this criterion.

Another structural aspect of a group is its size. This is limited by the number of members who can interact with each other. Very large groups simply cannot function as groups in themselves; they break up into smaller subgroups for purposes of accomplishing functions. Division of labor frequently occurs here with respect to the overall group task.

In addition to some kind of structure, whether formal or informal, all groups have shared sets of attitudes, values, etc., and must serve important functions for their members. The stated function of the group need not be the primary function served for each member. For example, the stated function of a university class is education on a particular subject. However, the class may also serve other needs of the students, such as a place for making friends or meeting dates, a laboratory for practicing social skills, job advancement and social status (if not through this particular class, then through the degree to which this class will contribute) or even a hiatus from meeting the "real world." These secondary functions of the class may exceed the stated primary function in importance for many students. This especially became evident during the Vietnam War, when enrollment in college courses offered men a temporary refuge from the draft; often, they enrolled solely for this purpose. The functions served need not be identical for all members, either. For example, one student may be concerned with the benefits the course will offer for future employment, while another may view the class primarily as a social outlet.

Neither the structure nor the function need be stated specifically. In informal groups, such as groups of friends, the structure may be unspecified but still exist, i.e., one person has a car, another is very knowledgeable, another is good to confide in, etc. Similarly, the unstated ideology or shared values may hold just as rigidly as if it were stated, e.g., group approval/disapproval over choice of friends. As such, a distinction between formal and informal groups does not seem highly relevant.

All groups are not created equal, at least with respect to any given individual. Some groups will influence the individual much more heavily than others. For example, one might expect the opinions of a person's family to carry more weight in a given decision than the opinions of the person's swimming class. A group that the person will use as a point of reference in forming judgments and deciding behavior is called a reference group. The person need not conform to the standards of the reference group; he/she need only use it as reference. In fact, some reference groups may provide guidance on how *not* to behave or believe, e.g., a Teamster union member considering a United

Farm Worker lettuce boycott. The person also need not actually belong to the reference group; consider the number of women who read the society columns to see what the latest Paris or New York fashions are. The reference groups will most likely influence a person's values and set of preferences.

THE EFFECTS OF GROUP INFLUENCE

There has been considerable research on the individual's conformity to group standards and/or pressure. The classic studies pertaining to this were done by Asch (1951). In a task which in the absence of group influence induced few errors, the mere presence of an erroneous majority resulted in a significant number of errors. The effect of the majority was not total, though, since more than two-thirds of the answers given remained correct and wide individual variation existed in tendencies to conform. Some subjects went with the majority nearly all the time while others remained independent throughout. Some were very confident in their judgments and others were highly doubtful.

A post-talk interview with the subjects uncovered varying reasons for their behavior. Within the independent subjects, some stayed with their minority judgment because they were sure they were right, others did it on philosophical grounds of being an individual, while others weren't sure but tried to perform the task to the best of their ability.

The subjects who went with the (unanimous) erroneous majority more than half the time seemed to fall into three categories. Some actually perceived themselves that the majority opinion was correct and were not even aware of any group influence. Most of the yielders did so out of lack of confidence in their own judgment; they reasoned that everyone else can't be wrong. There was a third group, however, who knew throughout that their judgment was correct and that of the group was wrong, but they answered with the group because of their need not to appear different or inferior to the others. They yielded knowing what they were doing.

Asch considered several variations on the original experiment. He found that having the support of even one other person significantly decreased the yielding and in some cases eliminated it. A large psychological difference exists between being totally alone and having some minimum of human support. When this supporter deserted, the conforming to the majority returned in full force.

If the supporter did not immediately show this support but did so later, the yielding decreased, but the previously yielding subjects still did so more frequently than the subjects who originally yielded less often. If no one supported the subject's judgment but another person made less extreme errors than the majority, the overall yielding by the subject did not significantly decrease but the errors made now became those of the moderate-error person.

Asch also varied the size of the majority. For these experiments, the majority effect was zero with one opponent and reached full effect with three opponents. Yielding did not significantly increase with a larger majority.

Asch concluded that both independence and yielding in a given situation were a joint function of (1) the character of the stimulus (if the matter is unclear, there is greater reliance on majority judgments), (2) the character of the group forces (unanimity, size, etc.) and (3) the character of the individual (since even in the same experimental situation sizable differences existed in yielding behavior among individuals).

Venkatesan (1966) extended Asch's paradigm to include a situation in which the subject is made aware of the pressure to conform. In such cases, the subject reacted to the situation by showing independent judgment, compared to the situations in which the group norm was established without pressure.

Bourne (1965) examined the types of products on which reference group influence could be expected to operate. The underlying theme found was that the conspicuousness of the product or attribute of the product made its purchase more susceptible to reference group influence. Reference group influence could also vary depending on how secure the individual feels as a member of the reference group, the individual's perception of the group position and his/her own knowledge concerning the issue.

TYPES OF REFERENCE GROUPS

Family

A major reference group is, obviously, the family. A family has established norms of behavior and there exists a high degree of conformity to those norms by the members. The person need not feel pressure; Asch's (1951) yielders included those individuals who automatically adopted the perception of the group and those who relied on the judgment of the group, as well as those who conformed for conformity's sake. The family will be discussed in greater detail when exchange theory is considered.

Social Class

Another kind of reference group the person may have is his/her social class. The hierarchy of social classes reflects the stratification of a society by social prestige. Occupation seems to carry more weight than income in determining a person's social class. For example, ministers and school teachers have relatively high prestige but little pay, while plumbers and electricians may make good wages but are not considered in the ranks of the elite. However, a strong correlation between occupation and income does exist.

Different systems of social classes have been proposed. One of the older systems, that of Warner et al. (1960), proposes six major social classes:

(1) The upper-class is the "old blood" aristocracy. They have great wealth and their wealth has been in the family for two or three generations. They form the membership of exclusive clubs and schools, and are often those featured on the society pages of a newspaper.

(2) The lower-upper class is the "nouveau riche," those who have only recently acquired their money. They are wealthy but not fully accepted socially in the ranks of the upper-upper class. Owners of large businesses, top executives and some high-salaried professionals are included in this category.

(3) The upper-middle class consists largely of professionals and managers. This class often provides the leadership of a community.

(4) The lower-middle class is comprised of white-collar office workers, small-business proprietors and some highly skilled blue-collar workers.

(5) The upper-lower class is the "working class" of the blue collar workers. Basically, this class consists of those who make a living by working with their hands.

(6) The lower-lower class contains the disreputable elements of society, especially the hard-core unemployed and those living on a slum-level existence.

Some disagreement exists among sociologists concerning the descriptions of the lowest classes, such as whether unskilled labor belongs in the lower-lower or upper-lower class. Others include a middle-middle class in the system and more finely sort the middle-class occupations. This could be justified by the increase in numbers of the middle class in recent years.

Another method of determining social class is to ask the people themselves which class they are in. The proponents of this method argue that the way in which people perceive themselves will better predict their behavior than will their designation by an outside observer. Under this method, a larger percentage of people call themselves middle-class than one might expect from objective classifications. Further, this percentage seems to have increased over time (Centers 1952; Morris and Jeffries 1970).

Members of social classes also have certain perceptions of members of other classes (Davis et al. 1941). In general, members of a certain class would have a fairly good opinion of their own class and see the class immediately below them as being less fortunate than they; however, they see the class immediately above them as being snobbish and giving themselves pretensions of grandeur. The classes far distant from the social class considered blend together in the observer's eyes. They are simply too alien from the given class for the fine distinctions and strong opinions to be formed. This could have implications for behavior; if a particular product or activity has a strong association with a particular social class, people might react to the product on the basis of their feelings about the social class.

The underlying presumption concerning the relevance of social class behavior is that placement within a social class will result in consistencies among those members in values. Assuming that the models to which a child is exposed are primarily members of his/her own social class, this may be due to observational learning. Much of the observational learning research has been concerned with the learning of values. This will yield consistencies in lifestyles, which in turn will lead to consistencies in behavior, including consumption behavior. These consistencies, especially those in consumption, have been extensively documented by sociologists and marketers (Levy 1966).

One might expect the norm thus established for a class to be followed by its members, or those who aspire to membership, as a result of conformity. For example, differences exist among the classes in values for education and deferred gratification. Values for education influence the consumption of college courses and ultimately income and upward class mobility. Values for deferred gratification affect not only present product consumption but credit patterns (Mathews and Slocum 1969), and again ultimately the means with which to move into another class. As such, the process becomes circular; not only do the consequences of class placement include behavior, but behavior patterns influence class mobility. As a result of the learned preferences, the person makes a choice which then has repercussions for future choices. These examples relate to investment goods, the choice of which affects the budget line through effects on future income.

The possibility of social mobility itself affects behavior. In a society which has a high degree of socioeconomic inequality, and presumably confers status on an achieved rather than ascribed basis so mobility is possible, greater risk-taking behavior occurs as compared to an egalitarian society (Pryor 1976). People who see the possibility of advancing in status may well take a gamble in order to achieve it. If, however, they already barely subsist, any loss would have disasterous consequences and a gamble would not be taken. The person would have preferences among the alternatives involved in the gamble, heightened in this instance by the connotations of those alternatives in terms of social status. The risk involved refers back to the budget line constraint.

Culture

The culture of the society in which a person lives also has a substantial impact on his/her beliefs and attitudes. Several definitions of culture have been proposed. According to Krech *et al.* (1962), the culture of a people consists of their distinctive modal patterns of behavior and the underlying regulatory beliefs, norms and premises. He sees culture as ways society develops to cope with common problems which then are transmitted to future generations. Ways of coping with problems involve the symbols of language, technology, roles and shared beliefs, norms, rules of behavior, and values.

The above view of culture contains some important aspects. First of all, culture continually changes because it develops through the interaction of the members of a society. Human interaction is in itself a dynamic, not a static process. Therefore, the results of this interaction should not be static. Ideas, symbolic interpretations and customs, all of which constitute aspects of a culture, change over time. For example, two hundred years ago in the United States, the words "madam" and "mistress" had considerably different connotations than they do now. As was discussed under the symbolic interaction theory of the self, the changing of shared interpretations of symbols and gestures can have considerable importance for the way in which a person develops.

Second, culture is learned, not innate. The process of learning a culture is called socialization. Some of the ways previously discussed in which socialization might take place include observational learning to acquire the culture and learn to perform in accordance with the reinforcement seen given to others, and conformity pressure to continue to behave in accordance with the surrounding society. The person is also often explicitly taught via language the meaning of gestures in a society.

Consequences of this include the function of social control which culture serves. As mentioned previously, groups, including societies, function much more smoothly if they have well-defined roles and the occupants of those roles behave in accordance with expectations. This must restrict to some extent the freedom of the individual. However, although culture serves as a constraint, it is an internal constraint rather than an external one. For the individual in the indifference-curve analysis, culture works on the individual's set of preferences instead of affecting the budget line which is the perceived situational constraint. The person has learned these preferences at least partly on the basis of cultural influence. Often, the individual is not even aware that culture has had this influence. This individual has internalized the culture. Again, this internalization may be accomplished through the effect of culture on the person's learned beliefs and values, through reference group influence (whether felt or not) and through the self (in this case, the identity) which the person has acquired on the basis of interaction with other people. This does not imply that all members of a society are alike; the unique combinations of demographic types of variables such as race, religion, social class, sex and heredity will affect responses to and responses from others.

Subcultures reflect some of these demographic groupings within the overall culture. For example, ethnic groups tend to have distinctive traditions or ways in which previous generations coped with societal problems. A person born into one of these groups will be socialized into the ways of his/her group, since other members of the group will likely be those with whom he/she associates most frequently. The same reasoning applies to other types of subcultures, such as race, religion, age, region and urban/rural lifestyles. Correlations between demographic variables, i.e., region and urban/rural living, and between these and social class, i.e., religion and social class, strengthen the probability of distinctive behavioral patterns.

Effects of culture on behavior are too widespread to necessitate their elaboration. In consumption behavior alone, products and activities carry different connotations in different cultures. For example, in the United States white teeth are valued while in Southeast Asia black teeth are beautiful. In France and Great Britain, shopping trips include much more social activity than in the United States. Pricing institutions also vary, from barter in some African societies to bargaining in others, to resale price maintenance to prices set by the seller. Ethnic groups within a given society have different consumption patterns; an Italian cook and a Chinese cook would come from the market with very different purchases. Differing religious doctrines frequently require distinctive consumption; consider, for example, the religious composition of the markets for rosaries, kosher meat and pork. The teenage subculture is noted for its consumption of cosmetics, records and some fashions.

Cultural change affects consumption and vice versa. For example, the shift in emphasis in the United States from production to consumption, particularly the increase in leisure time, has increased the number and variety of products consumed. Recreational products and activities especially have soared. Relaxed cultural values against debt have facilitated the growth in consumer credit. Conversely, a few major product innovations have had substantial impact on the culture; consider the automobile, the computer and more recently the birth control pill.

The relationship between product and culture involves the idea of consistency. New products will be more readily adopted the more closely they fit in with a prevailing culture or lifestyle (Graham 1954). Consistency also affects the development of the culture itself. New ways will tend to be those which are consistent with existing values. This partially results from existing perceptual organizations, as well as the discomfort which arises from cognitive inconsistency.

As such, the person's preferences or attitudes toward the elements involved in a decision are shaped by both the individual's own personality and the reactions of others in the society. The person must consider both his/her preferences and what he/she perceives to be possible in the situation in order to reach a decision. That decision will be the one which the individual perceives will maximize his/her satisfaction.

APPLICATION OF THEORIES

Symbolic Interaction and the Purchase of Records
by Kathleen S. Burton

In John W. Kinch's (1973) theory of self-concept, social interaction shapes the individual. Through a series of postulates, Kinch illustrates a circular pattern regarding the way in which an individual's self-concept affects and is affected by the responses of others. These "others" that Kinch speaks of refer to the "generalized other." The individual puts the responses of a group together as a whole, with some responses being very important and other responses being virtually ignored. The "generalized other" becomes the individual's impression of the group as a whole. Also, there is not just one group of others; there may be different groups which have effects on different areas of the individual's self-concept.

This paper will focus on Kinch's circular model as a means of analyzing a teenage consumer's decision for purchasing certain types of record albums. Kinch's model is as follows.

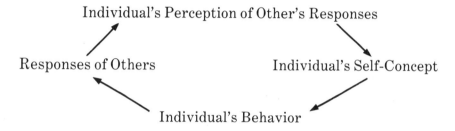

Individual's Perception of Other's Responses

Responses of Others   Individual's Self-Concept

Individual's Behavior

Kinch's first postulate is that the self-concept is based on the perceived responses of others. The teenager's self-concept of his/her taste in music is based on how he/she thinks others are reacting to him or her. In looking at this first postulate, it must be realized that there are some limitations. The person's self-concept does not change each time that someone responds to him/her differently. For example, the teenage consumer in question may believe that his/her taste in music is quite up-to-date and consistent with those in his/her peer group. If he/she believes that one friend is criticizing his/her record collection, it is doubtful that the teenager would change this self-concept and feel obligated to go buy a different kind of record. However, if he or she perceives that all of his/her friends are criticizing these records, he or she may begin to feel that his/her taste in music is not as good as he or she thought it was.

Another factor regarding the first postulate is the importance of those whose responses the individual is perceiving. For the teenager deciding on his/her taste in music, the peer group will most likely be the most important. If he/she feels that his/her parents or other adults don't appreciate his/her taste in music, it is doubtful that the teenager will try to change. In fact, criticism by adults may even serve to reinforce his/her self-concept about how good his/her taste in music is.

Kinch's second postulate says that the individual's self-concept functions to direct his/her behavior. If the teenager feels that he/she has good taste in music, he or she may purchase many albums. If he or she is less sure of his/her ability to recognize good music, he or she may be more hesitant about spending money on records. Also, this self-concept will affect the types of records purchased. If one perceives oneself as being very modern, one may decide to buy rock music; but if one perceives oneself as being intellectual, one may decide on something classical.

Kinch's third postulate is that the individual's perception of the responses of others toward him/her reflects the actual responses of others toward him/her. This means merely that the individual is relatively accurate in perceiving responses of others.

But there are five things that Kinch (1963) says can affect the individual's perception of others toward him or her. The first is the individual's familiarity with others. For example, the teenager may perceive a facial expression to mean something it doesn't mean in someone he or she may not know well. Second, the individual's familiarity with a situation affects his or her perception. If the teenager is used to playing his or her albums for one or two attentive friends, he or she may not understand why none of these friends pay attention to these records at a party. Third, the social visibility of the situation may have an effect. For example, the teenager may pay more attention to how a friend is responding to his or her albums in a group than he or she will when they are alone. Fourth, perceptions of others' responses vary with past experience in interpersonal situations. If the teenager has in the past found that a friend has similar tastes in music, he or she may fail to perceive that this friend actually dislikes his or her latest album. Fifth, other factors relating to all perception may affect an individual's perception of others' responses. For example, if tired, the teenager may perceive a neutral comment or expression as being unfavorable to his/her taste in music.

To complete Kinch's circular model, the fourth postulate states that the actual response of others is based on evaluative responses to the individual's behavior. The music that the teenager plays for various groups of people influences their response to him/her in regard to musical tastes. If the teenager always plays classical music to his/her friends, they may let him or her know that they think the teenager's taste in music is not up-to-date. On the other hand, his or her parents may express approval of the same records.

From these four basic postulates, Kinch came up with three others, but the circular effects that others' responses have on an individual's behavior and vice versa are found in the above-mentioned four. The teenager perceives something when others react to the albums he or she has purchased. From this perception comes his or her self-concept with regard to taste in music. This in turn affects the kinds of albums he or she will purchase in the future. And the kinds of albums he or she actually buys in the future will affect the way others will respond to him or her about his/her musical tastes. The individual's self-concept is not a static thing; as one displays new behaviors, others may react in different ways, thus possibly changing the individual's self-perception and future behavior. Although Kinch does not deny that there are other forces at work in the development of the individual, he sees group processes as an important factor in this development.

Social Influence and the Dieting Consumer
by Melanie Kickert

We live in an affluent society where every 1 out of 3 Americans is much heavier than he or she should be, with the percentage swelling rapidly (Anon. 1973A). Ever since we were small children we have been told to clean our plates, we have been overstuffed with junk food, and we have been conditioned to believe that apple pie is more appealing than green beans. The newspapers and television screens offer tantalizing foods tempting us to run for the refrigerator, but at the same time offer an even more persuasive message: be slender. "So all-persuasive is the media and fashion image of a trim, flat-bellied Mr. and Ms. America with their implied vigor and youthful, active sexuality that almost everyone feels compelled to try and measure up" (Anon. 1973A). The most recent Gallup poll showed that 1 out of every 3 Americans intended to go on a diet while only one-fifth had ever attempted to shed pounds (Anon. 1959). Accumulating excess pounds arises from fairly normal, as defined by our culture, eating habits. Thus dieting, for the majority of consumers, is viewed as undesirable. This author's concern is in focusing on the consumer who does diet and reasons why, thus consuming goods such as diet foods, diet books and artificial sweeteners in his/her quest for a slimmer body.

The food industry has profited greatly from the nation's obsession with weight loss. The total market, including foods, doctors who specialize in weight loss, health spas, exercise devices,etc., reached a soaring 10 billion dollars in 1973 (Anon. 1973A). Diet breads dominate the diet food market followed by slimming aids such as food substitutes or supplements, artificial drinks and artificial sweeteners and slimming tablets. There is a stagnation period in the market which reflects our cultural patterns, lasting from Thanksgiving until early spring. "Sales rise greatly in the spring when we shed our winter fat to flatter summer nakedness" (Anon. 1973A). Reader demand for the latest diet books has soared so that millions of copies of the several hundreds of diet books available will sell in a year alone. Diet books advocating anything from high-protein to hard boiled eggs and from fasting to a "sensible diet" sell like wildfire. These books include Dr. Irving Stillman's *The Doctor's Quick Weight Loss Diet* published in 1967, which has already sold five million copies, Jean Nidetch's *Weight Watcher's Cookbook* and the "granddaddy" of all diet books, Joe Moe's little red 25¢ booklet, *Calorie Counter and Control Over the Counter*, which since 1951 has sold 17 million copies (Anon. 1973A).

The slimming market is almost exclusively dominated by females. Dieting and being slim are a particularly female phenomena that have been exploited by manufacturers for some time. Eighty percent of the slimming food sales are made to women in the 25 to 45 age bracket. Dieting was previously an upper-class sport, but with prosperity following the Depression, the middle class could afford to to be fat, thus to diet. In 1964

(Blackwell *et al.* 1970) Mead Johnson, producers of diet products, completed a survey of their customers, classifying them as follows:

(1) married women,
(2) metropolitan area residents,
(3) middle to upper social classes,
(4) above average income,
(5) higher than average education,
(6) more likely than the general public to be a new product innovator,
(7) a spender as opposed to a saver, and
(8) age group 35 to 49.

Although men worry less about their weight than women do, medical authorities say that men are by far the better dieters. This has been attributed to the fact that more women diet for cosmetic reasons whereas more men diet for the purpose of good health. Other studies looking at who succeeds at dieting have found that people over 50 do poorly. The well-to-do are more likely to succeed at dieting than are the poor. People 60% overweight have a worse chance of losing weight. Singles under 30 stick to diets more easily than women who are widowed, divorced, or over 30, and those who are successful at dieting in their first week's attempt are more likely to continue with good results. Finally, those consumers with a low anxiety level who seldom suffer from depression have a better chance of shedding pounds (Anon. 1963).

Reference groups play a major role in influencing the dieter. Psychologists and anthropologists have grouped dieters and people who consume diet products into different categories. People in one such category, the "attention attracters," are strongly influenced by their peer group. This group encompasses young people who are susceptible to fads and other types of conformity and desire to attract attention. The norms of the reference group include slim figures and often fad diets which occassionally advocate only cottage cheese, toast or other such foods. This type of influence attracts attention to the fact that the individual is upholding the norms of the reference group. It may also be a device for the person who is overweight to attract the attention of friends. Often the participant seeks to be reassured that her appearance is good and that she does not need to diet.

A research study done by psychiatrist Kelly Brownell of Brown University's Butler Hospital's weight control clinic emphasizes that group support contributes to the dieter's success. The researchers recruited 38 overweight women, each at least 15 pounds overweight. The women were divided into three groups. One control group was told that they were on a waiting list for a weight loss program. The minimum contact group met six times in a 10 week period, while the other group of dieters met 16 times. Dieters were weighed at each meeting and received weight control manuals in the mail. At the end of 10 weeks, results showed that group contact greatly affected the success of the diet. The waiting list dieters gained an average of two pounds during 10 weeks. The minimum contact group lost an average of four pounds as opposed to the 10 pounds lost by the group with the most contact. Follow-up studies showed that women in the most contact group study successfully maintained their losses while women in the other groups gained pounds (Anon. 1973B).

The success of "Weight Watchers" further implies that dieters are more likely to succeed under the benefits of group support. The Weight Watchers program includes diet food manufactured by Weight Watchers, cookbooks, special diets and group meetings. Members converse about their weight problem in a group. Identifying with a reference group having common goals and a specific function contributes to the success of group dieters.

Learning and self-concept are closely integrated with an individual's desire to be slim and consume diet products. Through reinforcement, society teaches us what is an acceptable self-image to project. Women have learned through rejection and acceptance that weight deviations are more of a social liability for them than for men. A successful career man may be obese, but the successful woman can rarely take the same liberty. Consequently, appearance is more intertwined with the self-concept in females than in males. Looks are their whole personal value to many women who have never been encouraged to value themselves in any other way, so a gain in weight ties in directly with a reduction of their worth. Studies by Hueneman (Scott

1976) indicate that women weigh themselves more often than men and know their weight more constantly and consistently than men do. Further studies reflect social and sexual problems which arise for the overweight individual in fitting into our present, rigid cultural standards. Monello and Mayer (Scott 1976) found that obese girls showed personality characteristics such as passivity, obsessive concern with self-image, expectation of rejection and progressive withdrawal, all strikingly similar to the traits of ethnic and racial minority groups due to their status as victims of prejudice. It is no surprise that these women have pathetically negative self-images.

Most individuals view their ideal self as lithe and trim, fitting into the suggested norms of society. This self-concept arises from experiences which are both good and bad. We develop our real self or self-concept by storing the experiences we consider valid and by screening out the inconsistent ones. Society attaches a positive significance to the slender physique, so experiences associated with it demand a positive response. Consequently, the overweight individual acquires negative responses toward his/her appearance, thus, forming a negative self-concept concerning his/her weight. Since we strive toward our ideal self, or self that we would like to have, weight loss is obviously a means of attaining this.

Attitudes toward the self, like all attitudes, are learned. But why do we learn to strive for a slender self-concept? When people interact with one another, there is a natural interest in the appearance of the body that results in an interest in dieting. There is no innate reason why heavy people should be considered unattractive and in some societies, where there is a scarcity of food, obesity is a sign of prosperity and very desirable. In our culture, however, the slender figure is considered desirable for the person concerned with social interaction. Fashion and particularly the media promote the slender look. Corporations, secretarial schools, military organizations, TV commercials and magazines support being trim. Consequently, our cultural norm is a slender figure and acceptance of this norm often means dieting. Thus, the modern woman is trapped by this stereotype of femininity, which emphasizes her worth not usually for her intelligence, but for her bodily appearance. She can lose out on both sides; psychologically, if she feels her image is unsuitable, and socially, by the fact that slimness is the foremost way to be accepted.

Cultural values, attitudes and ways of satisfying personal and social needs are learned. Through a repeated pattern of reinforcement, we learn to strive for an image which society suggests. Learning theories, such as that proposed by Dollard and Miller (1956), stress how rewards and reinforcement lead an individual to behave in a manner conducive to purchasing diet foods and diet products. When a person responds toward adopting a thinner self by purchasing diet products and losing weight, society rewards the individual. These rewards may be in the form of attraction from the opposite sex, being able to wear the latest fashions, acceptance into certain groups and various compliments from all sides. This behavior is continually reinforced because our cultural norms are very rigid and offer little allowance to change. Rewards are the key to a dieter's behavior. A person will continue to respond in this manner because responses are a consequence of previous learning and responses leading to a trim figure merit positive reinforcement. Society offers negative responses toward the overweight individual, thus creating a great deal of anxiety for him or her.

In conclusion, I would like to cite the advertising campaign used by Mead Johnson (Blackwell *et al.* 1970) to promote "Metrecal," the diet milkshake. Mead Johnson's commercials display what we have learned to be appealing lifestyles and offer attractive people who represent an ideal self to the majority of society. Metrecal had previously been marketed using a medical approach which began to lose its sales effectiveness in 1964. The new marketing approach, which was highly successful, displayed attractive people in elegant dinner settings, active scuba diving scenes, or other situations made possible because the people consumed Metrecal at lunch. "Join the Metrecal for lunch bunch" became the new slogan, and ads displayed people having fun together. Typical copy referred to Metrecal in a "glorious lineup of nineteen wickedly rich creamy milkshake flavors." Acceptance into a reference group was another appeal offered by the approach. People were always shown in groups sharing common interests and activities. The success of the Metrecal advertising campaign supports the contribution of learning, self-concept and reference group acceptance to the consumer's purchase of slimming products. As long as our cultural norms remain consistent, dieting will continue to be a preoccupation within our society and diet products will continue to be success-fully marketed.

REFERENCES

ANON. 1963. Who succeeds in dieting? Sci. Digest (9).

ANON. 1973A. Dietmania. Newsweek, Sept. 10.

ANON. 1973B. Group dieting rituals. Society (1).

ASCH, S. 1951. Effects of group pressure upon the modification and distortion of judgments. In Groups, Leadership and Men. (H. Guetzkow, Editor.) Carnegie Press, Pittsburgh.

BLACKWELL, R. D. et al. 1970. Cases in Consumer Behavior. Holt, Rinehart and Winston, N.Y.

BOURNE, F. 1965. Group influence in marketing and public relations. In Dimensions of Consumer Behavior. (J. McNeal, Editor.) Appleton-Century-Crofts, New York.

CATTELL, R. and STICE, G. 1960. The Dimensions of Groups and Their Relations to the Behavior of Members, Inst. for Personality and Ability Testing, Champaign, Illinois.

CENTERS, R. 1952. The American class structure: A psychological analysis. In Readings in Social Psychology (rev. ed.) (C. Swanson et al., Editors.) Holt, Rinehart and Winston, New York.

COOLEY, C. 1930. Human Nature and the Social Order. Charles Scribner's Sons, New York.

DAVIS, A., GARDNER, B. and GARDNER, M. 1941. Deep South. University of Chicago Press, Chicago.

DOLLARD, J. and MILLER, N. 1950. Personality and Psychotherapy. McGraw-Hill, New York.

EITZEN, D. S. 1974. Social Structure and Social Problems in America. Allyn and Bacon, Boston.

GRAHAM, S. 1954. Cultural compatibility in the adoption of television. Soc. Forces 33, 166-170.

KASSARJIAN, H. and ROBERTSON, T. 1968. Perspectives in Consumer Behavior. Scott, Foresman, Glenview, Illinois.

KINCH, J. 1963. A formalized theory of the self-concept. Amer. J. Soc., 481-486.

KINCH, J. 1973. Social Psychology. McGraw-Hill, New York.

KRECH, D., CRUTCHFIELD, R. and BALLACHEY, E. 1962. Individual in Society. McGraw-Hill, New York.

LEVY, S. 1966. Social class and consumer behavior. *In* On Knowing the Consumer. (J. Newman, Editor.) John Wiley and Sons, New York.

MATHEWS, H. and SLOCUM, J. 1969. Social class and commercial bank credit card usage. J. Market. *33*, 71-78.

MELTZER, B. 1964. The Social Psychology of George Herbert Mead. Cntr. for Soc. Res., Western Michigan Univ., Kalamazoo.

MORRIS, R. and JEFFRIES, V. 1970. Class conflict: Forget it! Sociol. Soc. Res. *54*, 306-320.

PRYOR, F. 1976. The Friedman-Savage utility function in cross-cultural perspective. J. Pol. Econ. *84*, 821-834.

SCOTT, R. 1976. The Female Consumer. John Wiley and Sons, New York.

VENKATESAN, M. 1966. Experimental study of consumer behavior: Conformity and independence. J. Market. Res. *3*, 384-387.

WALKER, G. 1959. The great American dieting neurosis. N.Y. Times Mag., Aug. 23.

WARNER, W. L., MEEKER, M. and EELLS, K. 1960. Social Class in America. Harper and Row, New York.

7

After the Choice: Modifications of Attitudes/Response Sets/Perceptions

The story does not end when the person finally makes the choice. The decision will have repercussions on both attitudes/ response sets, via either cognitive or traditional learning theories, and on the person's perception of the situation. The effects on preference structure from both the behaviorist and attitudinal viewpoints will be considered and then the idea of the perceptual cycle previously discussed will be briefly reiterated.

LEARNING

A given choice or behavior will have implications for future behavior through the mechanisms of learning. A person learns through past experience and this learning will guide future experience. One manifestation of learning, personality, has already been discussed. The basic concepts of stimulus, response and reinforcement, including drive and cue, were outlined.

Learning theory rests on three basic assumptions. First, it assumes people are hedonistic. An individual will seek to gain pleasure and avoid pain. This is consistent with the maximization of satisfaction as previously discussed. Second, it assumes (more or less, later theorists less so) that learning occurs through the building of associations between stimulus and response or between stimuli. Third, it assumes that a person's behavior is determined basically by environmental factors, rather than hereditary or other innate factors.

These associations are acquired, in traditional learning theory, through conditioning. Classical conditioning depends on the mere closeness in time of an unconditioned stimulus, such as food, and a conditioned stimulus, such as a picture of food. If the conditioned and unconditioned stimuli are presented at the same time or nearly the same time, the person will eventually make the same response to the conditioned stimulus as to the unconditioned stimulus, even without the presence of the original stimulus. If the person responds with awakened appetite to the presence of food, and the food is always accompanied by its picture, eventually the picture of food will be sufficient to awaken his/her appetite. It is to be noted that this process does not require any conscious effort or other active participation by the person; the person is basically acted upon by the environment.

Instrumental conditioning, on the other hand, depends on the presence of a reward which the person receives as a consequence of a response. Instrumental conditioning occurs to the extent that this response which leads to the reward increases in the probability of its occurence. If no reward is received for a response, the tendency for that response to occur will lessen. As the name "instrumental conditioning" implies, the response is made as a means to the reward. This type of conditioning depends on the person making the response, without which no reward would be received and no learning would take place. The obtaining of the reward constitutes the reinforcement previously described.

The principles involved in conditioning and in more traditional theories of learning can be seen in the above types of conditioning. The earliest principle observed was that of contiguity, described in classical conditioning. Associations are acquired through the proximity of the elements in time or space. Thorndike (1913), while agreeing with the general principle of conti-guity, held that these associations so formed are strengthened by their repetition, rather than by mere contiguity as such. This he termed the "law of exercise." Two major implications develop from this. The first, the "law of use," is a restatement of the laws of exercise and contiguity; connections between a stimulus and a response or between two stimuli arise through their proximity to each other and are built up through repetition. The second, the "law of disuse," states that these connections will become weaker over time unless they are repeated or practiced.

The early researchers did not disagree on these principles. However, these proved to be more complicated than originally supposed. For example, the attention which a person devotes to an association, as well as the frequency with which it occurs, will influence its strength. Also, people do not respond identically, which suggests that other factors operate. As a result, more mechanisms were added to learning theory; chief among them was the effect of rewards (the "law of effect"), as incorporated in instrumental conditioning.

The original law of effect as stated by Thorndike (1932) held that reward will strengthen connections between stimulus and response, while punishment will weaken them. However, upon further investigation, punishment did not seem to have any effect. Thus, the law of effect became asymmetrical; while rewards always strengthen associations, punishment has little or no effect on the strength of these connections. This law of effect can be seen directly in consumer purchases and brand loyalty. If the consumer is satisfied with a product or brand, he/she will repeat its purchase; if not, he/she will not buy it again. This will have the result of strengthening the consumer's response set with respect to the product. Whether reinforce-ment constitutes drive reduction as discussed under personality formation is open to question. Hull (1939) and Dollard and Miller (1950) link the two, while Skinner (1953) defines reinforcement in terms of its effects on behavior which makes the intervening process (drive reduction) irrelevant.

The two major principles of Thorndike, then, were those of repetition (law of exercise) and reward (law of effect). Another related phenomenon which was observed concerned the spread of effect, from learning the given stimulus-response connection to learning other connections marginally related to those involved. For example, a person who learns that a given soft drink, e.g., Coke, can satisfy thirst may also learn that other soft drinks may do the same, which will strengthen not only the tendency to purchase the given soft drink but any soft drink when thirsty. The person has generalized the thirst-Coke connection to other drinks as well. Generalization may also be observed in problem solving; prior experience with similar problems aids in solving the present one.

The reverse of generalization is discrimination. If the person is accustomed to drinking either milk or orange juice in the morning and then develops an allergy to milk, the person will no longer be "rewarded" for drinking milk. The specificity of a thirst-drink connection has increased. Now, only orange juice is an appropriate response to a morning thirst. The person now discriminates between milk and orange juice as rewarded responses.

The extent to which a consumer's discrimination and generalization responses take place is partially determined by the nature of the goods involved. Generalized responses may best be made among highly substitutable goods, for example, the soft drinks. With discrimination, the goods become poorer substitutes for each other. This in turn affects the preference structure between goods and the elasticities of the goods as described earlier.

More recently, learning theory has involved theories of memory which depart from a strict stimulus-response association in attempting to explain the relationship between stimulus and response. Some of these take an information-processing approach, which was described earlier in relation to an individual's acquisition of information. Under these, the person's present behavior may serve as a source of information for future decisions by affecting the information in the person's memory. This more properly fits under effects on perceived situational constraints. However, the person may acquire information concerning his/her preferences in the same way, which will affect the preference structure.

ATTITUDE CHANGE

From the other perspective, a person's preference is expressed in a set of attitudes. Not only may attitudes affect behavior, as previously discussed, but behavior may affect attitudes—which in turn should affect future behavior.

The basic premise is that the person will strive for consistency between attitudes and behavior or between different attitudes. Inconsistency creates a state of tension, sometimes termed "dissonance," which is uncomfortable for the person and which the person will therefore try to reduce. Inconsistency is likely to be realized only in the context of some situation or choice the person is making. In fact, many times a person becomes aware of inconsistency only after he/she has performed some behavior. If the inconsistency is between two attitudes, the person may compartmentalize them, i.e., refuse to see them as related and inconsistent, or change an attitude. If the inconsistency is between attitude and behavior, the person may either change the behavior, or, if that is impossible, change the attitude.

Balance Theory: Heider

Several theoretical models of attitude change have been proposed. One of the earliest, Heider's balance model (1946), was concerned with inconsistencies in a person's attitudes toward other people and the environment (Fig. 7.1).

Let P represent the person with whom the analysis is concerned. O is another person, and X is some object in the environment. Heider considered two types of relations, those of liking and unit (which represents association). The degree of liking or association cannot be represented; these relations are all-or-nothing, either positive or negative.

A balanced (equilibrium) state is achieved when all three relations connecting P, O and X are positive or two are negative and one is positive. Examples of balanced states are given in Fig. 7.1.

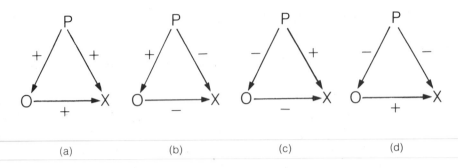

FIG. 7.1.   EXAMPLES OF BALANCED STATE

Suppose the three elements consist of the person (P), a close friend (O) and a certain car the person is considering purchasing (X). If the person and the friend are in agreement over liking (a) or disliking (b) the car, all is well. If the person no longer likes the friend or respects the friend's opinion and they are in disagreement over the car (c and d), again no problem arises. The person may disagree with everything this disliked other person says and remain comfortable.

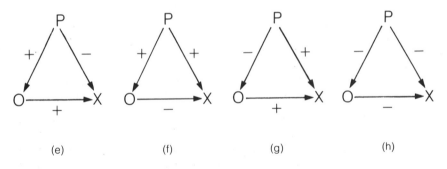

FIG. 7.2.   EXAMPLES OF UNBALANCED STATE

When disagreement exists with someone the person likes and whose opinion the person respects over an object (say, the car) as in (e) and (f), some tension also exists (Fig. 7.2). All is not harmonious. The person may resolve this by either changing his/her opinion of the car to agree with the friend's, or lowering his/her evaluation of the friend. In (g), the person finds him/herself in unexpected agreement with someone he/she dislikes. While support may not be unpleasant, it is inconsistent with the person's negative image of the other person and indicates a rethinking of attitudes may be in order. Therefore, this situation is not in equilibrium. Situation (h) is also unbalanced; if two people share an attitude, this gives rise to some common ground between them and at least some amount of liking on that basis; if nothing else, a grudgingly good opinion of the other person's judgment on this one issue. As such, incentives also exist for situation (h) to change to an equilibrium.

An unbalanced state creates some tension for the person, and as such gives the person some incentive to change one or more attitudes. Jordan (1953), in a test of this model, found that unbalanced situations were more unpleasant than balanced situations.

The Heider model has its limitations. It is not geared for more than two elements in addition to the person involved. It also does not specify the degree of liking or association; this is an all-or-none situation. Also, it does not take into account different kinds of liking; for example, two close girlfriends may be in love with the same man, which by Heider's model is balanced, yet one would not expect it to be a comfortable situation.

Balance Theory: Rosenberg and Abelson

A more general version of balance theory is that of Rosenberg and Abelson (1960). They remove the person involved as an element from analysis and consider the relevant elements, relationships between them and the person's attitude toward each element. As such, their model can include many more than the two elements of Heider's model and is not limited to person-other-person-environment attitudes.

A balance model consists of "elements" and "relations" which link the elements. Cognitive elements are "things," either concrete or abstract, such as persons, traits, products and institutions. A person may value these elements either positively, negatively or with indifference. Indifference contains no distinct value either way; this case is theoretically rather uninteresting. Relations can be positive, negative or null. Positive relations (symbolized +) are associative bonds and include liking, similarity, implying and consistency. Negative relations

(−), the dissociative bonds, include dislike, detachment, estrangement, incompatibility and alternativity. Null relations (0) indicate no bond at all, and can include indifference and irrelevance. An example of a statement in a balance model could be: "Time at work (valued −) is alternative to (−) leisure time (valued +)." Rosenberg and Abelson's balance theory, like Heider's, does not specify the degree of positivity or negativity in the relationship; only the sign is important.

X^+	$+$	Y^+
X^+	0	Y^+
X^+	$-$	Y^-
X^+	0	Y^-
X^-	$+$	Y^-
X^-	0	Y^-

FIG. 7.3.

Equilibrium exists as long as positive or null relations link elements of identical sign, and negative or null relations link elements of opposite sign. For any two elements in equilibrium, one of the possibilities shown in Fig. 7.3 must hold. If the model contains more than two elements, equilibrium must exist for every pair. However, only if the person recognizes the imbalance must he/she resolve it; he/she does have the option of not thinking about it. We will assume that all imbalances must be resolved. To resolve an imbalance, either attitudes concerning values of elements or the perceived relationship between elements must change.

As an example, consider the welfare dilemma from the point of view of the receiver. There are three major elements: income (M), which is positively valued; pride (P) in oneself and environment, which is also positively valued; and accepting charity (C), which is negatively valued. Pride and charity are negatively related; there exists, especially in some sections of the country, a very strong feeling against taking charity from anyone. To do so, even out of necessity, goes "against the grain" and is extremely detrimental to personal pride. Pride and income are positively related, from both feelings of personal accomplishment and conspicuous consumption. Income and charity must be positively related by the very nature of the concept of charity (only tangible charity is considered here). This link causes the imbalance in the model (Fig. 7.4).

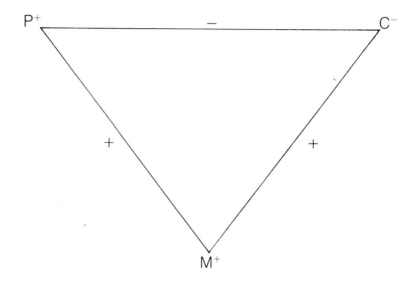

FIG. 7.4.   WELFARE DILEMMA

The simplest solution, reversing the link between income and charity, cannot be done. The individual by assumption will choose the path of least effort, making as few changes in values as possible. This rules out as too complicated the possibility of assigning negative values to P and M and making a positive link between P and C.

There remain four possible solutions to the Welfare Dilemma (Fig. 7.5). These cases are considered below:

Case I.   Place a negative value on M and create a negative relationship between P and M. This indicates that the person doesn't want income if any of it results from charity, and that accepting this type of income would be detrimental to a person's pride. This person, the traditional independent who

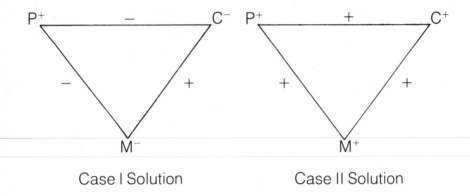

Case I Solution   Case II Solution

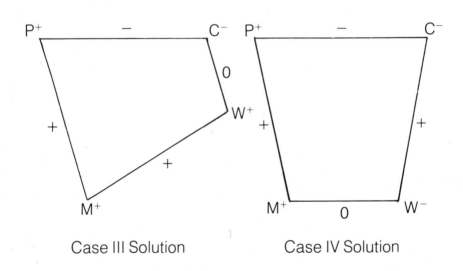

Case III Solution   Case IV Solution

FIG. 7.5.   POSSIBLE SOLUTIONS TO WELFARE DILEMMA

"won't take nothing from nobody," would rather starve than go on welfare.

Case II. Place a positive value on C and a positive relationship between C and P. Taking charity thus becomes positively valued and a source of pride for the person. The pride may come from "ripping off the system." This is the "demoralized" welfare recipient who has been socialized into the "welfare ethic" of "get all you can no matter how." Welfare cheaters fall into this category.

Case III. Dissociate "charity" from "welfare." In this way, the person still negatively values "charity," but now positively values "welfare" since it produces income. This person, probably the more usual welfare recipient, either does not or will not see welfare as charity. The extent to how well the person can dissociate could determine how resigned he/she is to being on welfare.

Case IV. Dissociate income due to charity (negatively valued) from income due to own efforts (positively valued). For example, income tax refunds are generally not considered charity although they come from the government on the basis of income and expenses. It is possible that the person would similarly dissociate a negative income tax scheme from charity. Case IV is the other extreme from Case I and in many ways resembles Case III.

One can also consider the balance theory version of the budget constraint (Fig. 7.6) and add this to the model (Fig. 7.7). Income, housing (H) (or any other basic good specified for analysis) and other goods (O) are all positively valued. Income is positively related to both H and O (assume both normal goods); H and O, because of the budget constraint, must be negatively related to each other. This creates another imbalance problem, which economic theory deals with so it will not be elaborated upon here. The combination of the Budget Dilemma and the Welfare Dilemma forms additional positive ties between P and both H and O. This becomes a sort of general equilibrium system

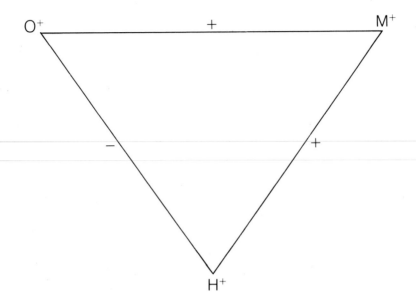

FIG. 7.6. BUDGET DILEMMA

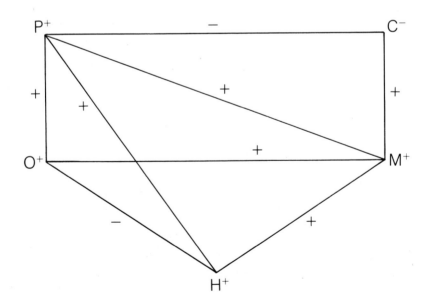

FIG. 7.7 COMBINED MODEL

in the person's mind. While one can make partial analyses, as economic theory does, such boundaries will be no more separable psychologically than are partial analyses in economic equilibria. Each case of the Welfare Dilemma will respond differently with respect to H to balance the total model. Because a positive relationship must in equilibrium connect elements of like sign, if the person perceives H as tied (+) to negatively valued charity the person will acquire a negative valuation of H.

As such, one can make a theoretical connection between a person's attitudes toward pride and welfare and his/her response to public assistance programs. By carrying the analysis through to specific goods involved, one could also see a relationship between the programs and the person's valuation (and possible later treatment) of the goods received. In general, goods which are directly tied to public assistance will be less favorably valued; this supports the implications from indifference-curve analysis that unconditional forms of assistance give the recipient the most satisfaction.

Congruity Theory

A special case of balance theory which does deal somewhat with the degree of positive or negative valuation is congruity theory (Osgood and Tannenbaum 1955). This deals with an individual's encounter with a statement about an issue and the person making that statement. The person will have attitudes toward both the issue and the speaker; the new connection between the two will influence the person's attitudes toward both.

The basic tendency presumed is toward polarization of attitudes; the person will desire maximum simplicity and an extreme attitude is simpler to maintain than an equivocal one. To illustrate this, Osgood and Tannenbaum use a congruity scale, along which subjects or speakers are aligned according to their polarization on some dimension.

The clearest example can be seen in politics. Consider the 1976 presidential campaign and a citizen's rankings of politicians and major issues along the liberalism-conservatism dimension. Suppose this citizen had the views as described:

George McGovern	+3	Abortion
Jimmy Carter	+2	Equal Rights Amendment
Gerald Ford	+1	Employment
John Doe	0	
George Wallace	−1	Neighborhood Schools
Barry Goldwater	−2	Defense Spending
Ronald Reagan	−3	Isolationism

If totally unknown John Doe took a position favoring abortion, John Doe would then be seen as extremely liberal. If Ronald Reagan introduced a new issue (initially neutral) into the campaign, that issue would take on the overtones of Reagan's political learnings. If Jimmy Carter made a statement supporting ERA, no change should occur; this statement would be expected of him. Similarly, no change should occur if Ronald Reagan attacked abortion or supported isolationism. In short, equilibrium exists when associative bonds connect equally polarized objects of like sign, i.e., speaker supports issue, or dissociative bonds connect equally polarized objects of opposite sign, i.e., speaker attacks issue. Reagan support of isolationism illustrates the former; Reagan attack on abortion illustrates the latter.

If Jimmy Carter made a statement supporting abortion, the model is not in equilibrium. Both the attitudes toward Carter and toward abortion will change; the reasoning works two ways. If Carter made such a statement on an extremely liberal issue, the citizen will start to think maybe Carter is more liberal than he/she thought. At the same time, if that issue is supported by Carter, who was known to be only moderately liberal, perhaps support of abortion is not such a liberal position as was previously thought. Therefore, Carter will be seen as slightly more liberal than before *and* abortion will be seen as a slightly more conservative issue. The rule concerning relative amounts of change in the two attitudes is that, since a tendency exists toward polarization, the more extreme of the two attitudes will change the least. By the formula Osgood and Tannenbaum present, both Carter and abortion would move to +2% on the scale.

Their formula divides the distance either element would have to move alone to restore balance according to the respective polarizations of the elements. For the issue:

$$\text{movement} = \frac{|S|}{|O| + |S|} \, |P|, \text{ where } |O| \text{ is the absolute value of}$$

the issue's scale positions and $|S|$ is that of the source; $|P|$ the distance either would have to move singly. For the source:

$$\text{movement} = \frac{|O|}{|O| + |S|} \, |P|, \text{ with symbols defined as above.}$$

Consider another example: Suppose that for a dieting consumer, saccharin has the value of +3 and the Food and Drug Administration has a value of +2. Now the FDA bans saccharin. Saccharin now moves to +1 and the FDA to −1. As the FDA action created a dissociative bond between saccharin and the FDA, either element would have to move 5 steps if it had the total burden of restoring equilibrium. That distance was divided inversely with the respective polarizations; saccharin, the relatively more polarized (+3 vs +2), moved relatively less than did the FDA (2 vs 3).

Some qualifications exist to this congruity model. For example, to return to the political case, suppose Ronald Reagan made a statement supporting abortion. Many citizens would simply not believe Reagan could have said that, or if he did, that he could not have meant it. Therefore, a "correction for incredulity" is included in the model to handle these extreme cases. In general, while the numbers on the scale may be questioned empirically, the principles involved in the congruity model seem well supported.

Dissonance Theory

Cognitive dissonance theory deals with the effect of the person's own behavior on his/her attitudes. Again, the underlying principle is that inconsistency, at least in an important situation, produces dissonance which is uncomfortable and which the person will try to reduce. If the person cannot or would prefer not to change his/her behavior, then he/she will probably adjust an attitude to reduce inconsistency. Minimizing the importance of the whole situation will also reduce the magnitude of the dissonance created by it.

In fact, all decisions or choices involve some dissonance. No alternative is completely good or completely bad; in any choice, to reject one alternative is to reject some positive qualities in it, and to accept another alternative is to accept some negative qualities which it has. Therefore, in each decision, especially in close decisions, the person wonders to some degree "did I make the right choice?" To reduce this dissonance, the person will attempt to reassure him/herself that the decision was correct; this can be aided by selectively seeking new information to confirm one's judgment (Ehrlich 1957) or by dwelling on the attractive features of the chosen alternative to make it seem even more attractive. This process will take place to a greater extent the more similar the ratings of the choices and (as a result) the greater the dissonance.

For example, consider a person who must choose between a Ford Maverick, a Ford Pinto and a Chevrolet Chevette. The person is looking for gas mileage, comfort, sturdiness, price and reliability. The person may reject the Chevette if he/she considers it inferior to the Pinto on comfort, sturdiness and reliability while not significantly better on the other aspects. This decision would create relatively little dissonance, although the Chevette still has some very attractive features. However, suppose the Maverick-Pinto decision is much more difficult. The Maverick is a larger, sturdier car with a very good repair history. On the other hand, the Pinto has better gas mileage and a lower price. Rumor holds that the Maverick will soon leave the market. Suppose the person ends by choosing the Pinto. The person still has a lingering affection for the Maverick. The person will feel much more comfortable in the decision if he/she can convince him/herself that either the Pinto is in fact a superior car or that the attributes on the basis of which he/she chose the Pinto are the most important ones, for example, by reading articles on the rising cost of gasoline. In either case, the person will, after the decision, raise his/her opinion of the Pinto and/or lower his/her opinion of the Maverick, which will have the effect of justifying his/her decision and reducing the dissonance involved.[1]

The implications of dissonance theory also extend to the case where a person is somehow induced to behave inconsistently with his/her attitudes or beliefs. Again, the inconsistency creates dissonance which must be reduced. In most cases, the behavior cannot be revoked; therefore, the attitude changes in order to justify the behavior. The classic experiments on this are those by Festinger and Carlsmith (1959) on the greater attitude change involved with a lesser monetary reward for telling lies about a boring experiment, and Aronson and Mills (1959) on the correspondence between the severity of initiation and attraction for an extremely dull group. In each case, subjects were induced to act in a way which they later had some difficulty justifying to themselves. Those with the less adequate external rewards explanation in the first experiment, which resulted in more dissonance, and those who had the most at stake in the situation in the second, which also created more dissonance, had significantly more favorable attitudes toward a less-than-enjoyable situation than did others.

In an investigation of effects on cigarette smoking of dissonance created by the 1964 Surgeon General's report linking cigarette smoking to cancer, Kassarjian and Cohen (1965) hypothesized that four methods of dissonance reduction by smokers might occur. First of all, the smokers could change their behavior patterns of smoking, either by quitting or attempting to quit, or by switching to cigars or pipes which at that time had not been linked with cancer. The smokers could also simply refuse to believe the report, or at least that they personally could be affected. Another strategy would be to minimize the importance of the health issue by accepting "lots of things are hazards," etc.; still another would be to seek new evidence supporting smoking, either in the form of other test results or in social support. The results of Kassarjian and Cohen's work indicated that smokers did everything except change their behavior.

---

[1] The reader should not construe this paragraph as an endorsement of any make or model of car.

Mittelstaedt (1966) asked whether dissonance reduction has any effect on the development of brand loyalty. In an experimentally manipulated situation, the resolution of a high dissonance situation frequently resulted in the later repetition of this choice even over a previously higher ranked alternative; such was not the case in a low dissonance situation.

An alternative to dissonance theory was developed by Bem (1967), who holds that attitudes are inferred from behavior rather than behavior from attitudes. A person will first of all behave in a certain way. When forced to become conscious of it, the person can look to either the situation or him/herself for explanations. If the situational reasons are not strong enough, the person will reason "well, I acted in this way without outside inducement, so I guess I believe this way." Bem argues that when others watch and interpret our behavior, they use the same reasoning process (attribution) as we do. For example, if one person is asked if another enjoyed a dinner, the answer may be "I guess so, he ate it all." Bem replicated the Festinger and Carlsmith (1959) study, yielding this conclusion. His explanation of the Festinger and Carlsmith results, however, differed from that of the dissonance theorists. Bem argued that the subjects, in informing others that a boring task was interesting, did not necessarily lie. They may have had no previous attitude toward the task. Those offered the lesser amount of money to "lie" decided that this money, the situational reason, was not sufficient inducement so they must have had a favorable attitude. Those offered the greater amount of money had a stronger situational reason for their behavior and so had no need to infer a positive attitude. Bem's approach views the individual as a problem solver rather than as a tension-reducer. Attributions tend to be made on the basis of covariance of actions over time, with other actions and in different settings.

Although widely researched, neither dissonance nor attribution theory nor a few other variations on them is easily defined, proved or disproved. Alternative explanations exist for most findings; disagreement within the psychological literature is rampant. They do agree that the person's actual behavior will have repercussions on his/her attitudes.

PERCEPTUAL CHANGE

The behavior by the person may affect not only his/her attitudes, but also his/her perception of the situation. One group of attitude change theorists, including Sherif *et al.* (1965), hold that this indeed happens. When a person makes one judgment and later seems to change that position, and the person is asked about the change, the person may well answer that the situation proved not to be as he/she originally thought. For example, a lifelong Democrat who votes for a Republican may say that this particular Republican has turned out more liberal than the voter thought at first. The person's attitude toward an object, in this case the person's attitudes toward liberals and conservatives, has not changed; the person's perception of the object itself has changed, in this case his/her perceptions of the candidates as being liberal or conservative.

This rests upon the factors involved in perception itself. The need for organization in perception, selectivity in perception and Neisser's (1976) schemata as the sets of expectations which help organize and govern what is perceived have been discussed previously. This schematic organization may change with experience; the schema accepts and is changed by information as information becomes available to the senses. The schema directs movements and exploratory activities that make more information available, by which it is further modified.

This has considerable implications for the person; although perceiving does not change the world, it does change the perceiver (Neisser 1976). The schema undergoes what Piaget calls "accommodation," and so does the perceiver. The person has become what he/she is by virtue of what he/she has perceived and done in the past, and he/she further alters him/herself by what he/she perceives and does in the present (Neisser 1976).

As such, the person's present experience of the world, acquired through behavior, modifies his/her expectations concerning the world, which in turn influence not only his/her perception of "reality" on which he/she will next act, but as a result, his/her future behavior.

APPLICATION OF THEORIES

Learning Theory: Children and Television Advertisements
by Elzora Dalrymple

Television is the first medium to treat all children as miniature consumers and to advertise to them on their own programs. Each and every Saturday morning about "50% of all the nations two to 11 year-olds are in place before their television sets" (Efron 1969). Even at that age they comprise an important market in the great American mercantile structure. Where a market exists in the inexorable logic of free enterprise, goods and services materialize to tantalize its special tastes. Children are promised popularity in their neighborhood if they buy a certain toy, are told they can grow big and strong by eating one brand of bread, and are offered excitement and adventure if they eat a certain candy bar.

Young children, many beginning at 18 months of age (Murray 1973), are attentive to television material. Preschool children watch three hours of television a day, and school children a little less. Research that was carried out while the educational series *Sesame Street* was being designed showed that commercials were consistently attractive to three to five year-old age groups. This is important because every encounter with the environment is a learning experience, and television forms an important part of the preschooler's environment. Anything that attracts a child's attention is a learning experience. According to Lesser (1974), there is no reason to believe that children do not learn from the advertisements if they are successfully attracted to them.

Attributes that are often present in commercials are the ones adopted for use in the format and teaching strategy of *Sesame Street*. They include: action that is directly relevant to the narrative; surprise, magic, suspense; action imperatives; a personal focus; lively rhythm and rhyme; and the use of children and cartoon characters. Attributes which are seldom present in commercials are the ones that most consistently cause children to "turn off." These include message monologues (talking heads), sound track unrelated to the visual action and ill-defined characters.

Not only the attractive appearance of commercials but their communication strategies as well prove handy in reaching children. Successful advertisements are educational in the strongest sense. They not only add to the store of information, but they may actually change behavior—they may cause a child to need or want something they did not need or want before.

Advertisers tap into the young child's voluntary tendency to watch television. Young children are creatures whose primary goal in life is to learn. They don't seek out television to alleviate boredom when they are very young. They watch television to learn and help them master their environment. The things they learn from a MacDonald's Hamburger advertisement are just as welcome as the ABC's. "*Sesame Street* gave the first real evidence beyond scattered anecdotes from parents of the remarkable rate at which children can learn from television" (Lesser 1974).

Learning is a multi-faceted process. Hilgard (1966) states that "learning brings about changes in behavior that result from previous behavior in similar situations, and that it is an important variable in and determinant of consumer behavior." Children not only learn a variety of things from television, but they learn them in a variety of ways. It was widely thought that young children could not be expected to learn very much without direct experience. The idea was generally reinforced by learning theorists stressing the role of tangible reinforcement in learning. It is now clear, based on the *Sesame Street* success, that learning in the absence of "hands on" experience, and in the absence of direct reward or punishment, happens in quite young children.

Miller and Dollard have predicted a theory of social learning concerning imitation upon a Hullian type of learning model. Hullian models involve both association and reinforcement. The principal mechanisms of Hullian learning models are drive, cue, reinforcement and reward, producing a response. Drive refers to an internal state of tension which calls for action. Cue is an environmental stimulus. Response represents the person's reaction to cues within his/her environment. Reinforcement happens to the extent that a response is rewarded. Reward is the goal object that satisfies the physiological or psychological need. The basic assumption is that all forms of human behavior are learned: to comprehend the complexity of behavior one must know the psychological principles involved in its learning and the social condition under which this learning took place. Learning via imitation constitutes the basic principle of this approach, which suggests a formidable model for consumer behavior and learning (Markin 1974).

Children develop the capacity for imitation of a model quite early (Fowles and Voyat 1974). They are able to learn from imitating the behavior of others in their presence, or those individuals observed by them through the media. The term "models" is used for individuals whose behavior children can observe, whether these individuals are personally in the child's presence or are conveyed through television.

Television has greatly increased the models available to children, not only in the areas of sex typing and dress, but in the exercise of self-control and inhibition (or disinhibition) of behavior. Imitation is an important process because "observational learning does not require direct teaching in order to be effective" (Lesser 1974). Learning is facilitated simply by observation of the model's response, whether or not reinforcement results from it. Bandura (1963) contends that an individual's response to cues in a stimulus field leads to internalized imagined responses in the observer that can be retrieved when the observer is placed in a behavior field. That is, a child can observe a performance, store it mentally and reproduce it later when the model is no longer present. Therefore, a child without being directly rewarded has the capacity to integrate the cue connections in a model's responses and becomes able to imitate the model's response.

Observational learning refers to the acquisition of knowledge through the viewing of the behaviors of others and the influence of that knowledge on one's attitudes and actions. Principles of observational learning are directly applicable to television because television involves exposure to the behavior of others as modeled on the screen. Modelling is the primary means by which television can impart, very often unwillingly, what Gerbner

(1974) calls its hidden curriculum, "a set of messages about the culture that no one teaches but everyone learns." Many of these messages are presented in advertisements.

A factor involved in modelling is the identification with the model. The child will learn more if he/she can readily put him or herself in the protagonist's place. This is easiest when the protagonist is the same sex as the viewer. The effect is heightened if the consequences of the protagonist's behavior are evident to the viewer. This is described as vicarious reward or punishment. When a child sees a lonesome child become overwhelmed with friends by mixing up Kool-Aid in a commercial, he or she can associate him or herself with that child and with the reward of the friendships obtained through the products' use. Imitation also increases when the model is perceived to be a powerful figure from a child's point of view.

The presence of a prestigious model, an uncluttered format, motion and activity and a change of scenes aid the learning process. An additional factor that aids in the learning process is the ability to generalize. Children are able to extend from the examples they see in the first learning experience, to somewhat different contexts and situations. In a study by Poulos (1976) for the Federal Trade Commission it was found that a certain commercial had the tendency or capacity to lead children to mistakenly pick and consume plants that could be harmful to them. The study was based on a series of commercials designed to advertise a major brand of cereal, Grape Nuts. In the commercials the cereal was associated with wild-growing plants, thereby emphasizing the natural qualities of the cereal. In the course of four commercials, Euell Gibbons (prestigious model) is shown picking wild-growing berries, cattails and parts of pine trees, while observing that each is edible and by implication healthful. In some of the ads the red berries actually were put into a bowl of cereal.

A child who by chance sees more than one of the commercials in question may observe that various wild berries are edible. It would not be a difficult step for a child to extract the general rule that parts of many wild-growing plants are good for consumption, thereby generalizing from the commercials.

A test was devised showing the set of four ads to children and obtaining a measure both before and after viewing of the adver-

tisements, of their beliefs about the edibility of a variety of
plants. They were asked to indicate whether the plant was good
or bad to eat. After the test was given to the children, ranging in
age from five to 11, the results showed that the advertisements
had little effect on the children's judgments of familiar edibles as
carrots or blackberries. On the other hand, the commercials did
have an influence on children's judgments of unfamiliar and in
fact nonedible plants. The effect was greatest for the plants
most similar in the pictures shown in the test, to those shown in
the commercials. This is consistent with what is known about
learning in general; the closer the new situation is to the original
situation, the stronger the learning effect. The results suggest
that the cereal commercials had the capacity to lead children to
engage in behavior that increases risks to their health.

Modelling is not the only mechanism that explains how young
children learn so much from television advertisements. Sheer
rote verbal learning is another. With repeated exposure, children can learn verbal chains such as song lyrics, or advertiser's
jingles and slogans. Music facilitates this process by providing
memory cues. As to the role of music, Helitzer (1970) says
children "will sing the words to commercials, clap hands to the
rhythm, mimic sound effects, and even dance to the commercial
music; although admittedly the younger the child is the easier it
is to involve them." Often what is learned in this way can be
trivial, but sometimes such a verbal chain can be associated with
a set of concepts or symbols and serves to organize them. With
television this is quite easy to bring about, since visual stimuli
can be presented in planned synchrony with their verbal corre-
spondents. For example, a certain cereal box can be shown while
a jingle containing its name is sung.

Television production can also be designed to bring more
elaborate cognitive processes into play. For example, a television scene may present an incongruity or unexpected incident
which will engage the child's mind. Consider the following segment from *Sesame Street*:

Two muppets, Bert and Ernie are involved. Bert in an effort
to establish his exclusive right to the cookie cabinet has painted
a "B" on its front doors. Ernie notices the letter spans the
divisions between the doors and in apparently innocent elaboration, establishes that the initial on the door determines access to

the cookies inside. Bert agrees. Ernie then opens wide the right hand door, removing the bumps from the "B" and leaving an "E" for Ernie, and helps himself to a snack. Here the letter becomes the center of attention, and the child is led to reflect on the critical differences between an "E" and a "B" (the bumps) while at the same time enjoying Ernie's joke on Bert (Palmer *et al.* 1975).

These are, of course, not all the learning processes involved in television programming and advertisements, but do serve to indicate the range.

Problems in advertising to children arise because they are a special audience. Children's attention patterns and reasoning processes are distinctly and qualitatively different from those of adults, so their ways of processing, perceiving and dealing with information are distinctly different from those of adults.

In all aspects of development children proceed through a series of distinct stages. The ability to think logically does not emerge until about age 12. Before that the child's thinking is at first intuitive, magical and egocentric, and then concrete and practical (Piaget 1970).

A child in the intuitive stage of intelligence, a preschooler, does not for example draw a clear distinction between his or her point of view and that of others. Likewise he/she does not discriminate between fantasies and objective reality. Dreams and imaginings have the status of observations. Logical necessities are not differentiated from events that are merely probable. The child at this stage cannot follow a line of inference, or a lengthy narrative, but views the world, including the television world, as a series of isolated incidents; nor can he/she incorporate concepts communicated only verbally. Clearly what a child takes, at this age, from a television advertisement will be quite different than what adults take away, or than what an older child takes away. Even a child of seven or eight is different from an adult, although increasing verbal skills may obscure all the differences. At this stage the child is still operating at a very concrete and literal level.

If there is a great potential for communication there is an equal one for miscommunication. Children are unpredictable in what they will pick up from a program or television commercial. Children use language differently from adults. Although they may use the same words as adults do, their feelings and understandings about words are different. Children are thus apt to misinterpret information in advertisements. In a pilot study (Kaye 1974), a television commercial for a children's game called "The Secret of the Missing Mummy" was shown to a group of preschool children, followed by a few simple questions about what the commercial showed. Many of the very young children were disturbed by the commercial because they assumed that the game referred to their own mothers who were missing. When asked why the mummy was missing, one child replied, "because she is making peanut butter and jelly sandwiches."

Children cannot think in an orderly fashion since they can't rehearse in their heads or try different solutions or free themselves from their personal interpretations of things. They cannot as easily separate fantasy and reality. For many young children, television is the real world. When one nursery school teacher asked a young child, "Are Batman and Robin real or pretend?" He replied firmly, "Oh, no. They're real." Children are left to cope with a bewildering quantity of confusing information (Kaye 1974). For this reason, a child would not be able to analyze and judge an ad or to discount its extravagant claims.

Most commercials are delivered by adults, and children are especially susceptible to favorite host characters whom they trust. Dr. Freda Rabelsky comments that children look to adults to find out what is "good" and "bad." Experiments with children report that children are concerned with what adults do and say, even strange adults whom they will never see again (Kaye 1974).

The child's learning during the first five or six years of life sets the foundation for lifelong patterns of behavior for further learning. Attitudes and values, as well as habits of thinking and reacting to others are set down during this formative period. Child psychiatrists and psychologists (Anon. 1970) think of the young child as especially susceptible to influence during the years of his/her life when he or she is dependent on other individuals for his or her growth and survival. A child has only a limited range of past experiences and does not have a well established set of conceptual categories for clarifying his or her perceptual experiences.

Because of their youth and inexperience, children are far more trusting and vulnerable to commercial pitches than adults.

There is evidence that very young children cannot distinguish conceptually between programming and commercials, and they do not understand that the purpose of a commercial is to sell a product. Ward (1972) found in a study of five to 12 year olds, that young children exhibit low awareness of the concept of commercials, frequently explaining them as part of the show or identifying them simply by naming a category of products. Older children exhibit greater awareness, explaining the commercials in terms of their purpose to sell, and discriminate between programs and commercials more readily than younger children. He also found that a child's distrust of commercials increases with age.

Researchers may assure the advertisers that the fixing of product preferences in childhood will guarantee consumer loyalty for a lifetime (Bliss 1967). Therefore, advertisers may try to use methods to attract a child's attention and make him/her want a specific product.

Some advertisers have done a much better job than others in creating commercials which advertise the brand rather than the product category. Some commercials make children want the specific object advertised (leading to a discriminating response), while others evoke a more generalized need that can be satisfied in a variety of ways. At one end of the scale are commercials for toys, and T.V. shows which almost invariably make the children want the specific toy or the specific entertainment. At the other end of the scale are the ads for ice cream and peanut butter which do little to create a preference for the advertised brand. Commercials for cereals fall toward the toy end of the scale, while commercials for cakes and cookies fall toward the peanut butter end (Well 1965).

Advertisers of products near the peanut butter end of the scale try to involve ways to individualize their brands and encourage brand loyalty. One of these ways is to offer prizes or premiums which can only be obtained through the use of their product. This tactic works in the sense that it makes children want a specific brand in order to get the prize. This tends to strengthen the cue. Post Cereals presently has a campaign working through the schools and the media using the premium concept. The children are encouraged to bring in box tops from the Post cereals and then they are redeemed with sports equipment for their schools. In a Northern Virginia grade school, for example, the principal communicated the message over the intercom system encouraging the children to participate. The children also saw advertisements on the television promoting this idea which further reinforced their response of asking their parents for Post cereals.

Another technique used is to make a child want a specific brand by the use of the emotional appeal of a magic power. Certain commercials imply that using the product will build muscles or increase athletic abilities. When asked directly about these claims, most children deny they believe them. But when the question is asked what commercials makes them want the product and why, the children respond "because it make you run fast." Wells (1965) concludes that the best hypothesis seems to be that on a rational level, children know the claims are not literally true, but the commercials have succeeded in creating an aura about the brand which gives the brand a special and highly desirable significance. The image is there even though the substance is not.

A somewhat more permanent solution to the individualization problem is to associate the brand with a personality the children admire. Because children do ask for certain brands just because the brands are identified with someone they like, this tactic is apt to remain effective as long as the personality remains popular. An example of this strategy is used by Del Monte vegetables in their commercials through the use of Bill Cosby.

Small children do not respond personally to television advertising. They cause their parents to purchase the advertised products. Central to the assessment of television's impact on children is the degree to which they are motivated to persuade their parents to buy advertised products. Helitzer (1970), an advertising executive writes of the persistence of children. "Children can be very effective naggers. By and large parents quite readily purchase products urged on them by their youngsters." He found that a parent will pay "20% more for an advertised product with child-appeal, even when a less expensive nonadvertised product is no different. 'Child-power' adds at least $30 million weekly or $1.5 billion annually, to grocery retail sales, just to make junior happy."

Goldberg and Gorn (1974) did a study centered around the question of to what extent television commercials motivate children to try to obtain advertised products. The study found that the chance or probability the child thinks he/she has of receiving the product advertised, influences the child's persistence in obtaining the product. For a variety of reasons, such as income and parental attitude, some children approach the viewing situation with higher expectancies of obtaining these products. The children with a higher expectancy perceived their chances of receiving the goods as significantly better than groups with a moderate or low level of expectancy, and worked the longest at an experimental task to win the toy. A child's behavior will also be influenced by the extent to which he/she values the product, goal object. A child will strive more for a product he or she likes more. The child's high expectancy of receiving the toy also influenced the value of the toy. The children who had a better chance of obtaining the toy liked it better and were more motivated to obtain it. The study also suggests that children value a product that is easier to obtain more than one that is harder to obtain. This differs somewhat from motivation studies where people value completion of a challenging task more than that of a successful completion of an easy task. The significant difference in the two examples is that the value of an extrinsic reward, the toy, is measured in Goldberg and Gorn's study, where in previous studies the value of an intrinsic reward, accomplishing the task, was measured.

The study also found that the repetition of commercial messages tended to enhance the product advertised and was consistent with Krugman's (1962) theory suggesting that the first three exposures to a stimulus are critical. Children who saw one commercial evaluated the advertised toy and worked harder at the experimental task to obtain it than those who did not see the commercial. Increasing the number of commercials from one to three did not significantly change either the attitude or behavior. This supports Krugman's idea that with the third exposure the viewer begins to disengage from what is perceived.

Goldberg and Gorn (1974) also found that those with no more than a moderate level of expectancy did not screen out the commercials. Thus, children with less of a chance of receiving the product were shown to still be affected by commercials.

Repetition in ads has two desirable effects. It fights forgetting, the tendency for learned responses to weaken in the absence of practice. It provides reinforcement after the purchase has been made because the consumer begins to selectively expose him or herself to advertisements of the product in order to reduce dissonance. Krugman (1965) states that "the public lets down its guard to the repetitive commercial use of the television medium and that it easily changes its ways of perceiving products and brands and its purchasing behavior without thinking very much about it."

Many of the patterns of consumer learning of children stems from the en-masse nature of ads. It is not the single ad for a toy or the isolated ad for a drug that changes a child's perspective. It is the 30 ads a day for toys or sweets or the 10 ads for drugs. Robertson and Rossiter (1974B) did a study oriented around a Christmas season, the peak season for toy and game commercials. They asked the children to nominate their Christmas present selection before the advertising campaigns began in early November and then after the campaigns in mid December. They found that children who had a high resistance to advertisements before the campaign, those who were skeptical of advertisements and had not chosen many advertised toys at the beginning of the peak period, by the end of the advertising campaign had had their defenses neutralized and were also responding to the television advertisements.

Wells (1965) found that the younger children were the less resistance they had to commercials. The younger respondents in his study, five, six and seven year olds, had little difficulty remembering and describing episodes in which they asked their parents for products they saw advertised on television. The items they mentioned most frequently were toys and breakfast cereals, which are the advertisements most heavily repeated during children's programs. Several children reported they asked for certain brands of dog food (for the dog). The older children described many fewer such requests. The 10, 11 and 12 year olds were more skeptical of television advertising, having found, they said, that things advertised on television do not always turn out to be as good as they appear. Thus, the simple, direct and overt "Mommy buy me..." response to advertisements seems to reach a peak in the elementary school years. Robertson and Rossiter (1974A) supported this same finding in their study of 289 boys. They found that the children were able to recognize commercial persuasion by the fifth grade. The child who is able to discern persuasive intent is less influenced by advertisements, less trusting of them, likes commercials less and makes fewer consumption requests.

The aspects of television advertisements for children that have so far received the attention of the researchers include the content of children's advertisements, children's reactions to commercials, their information processing of the commercial messages, their attitudes toward commercials, and their attempts to influence their parents to purchase the advertised product. Most of the data are based on interviews with children or their parents and are limited in size and in some cases sex. For example, in Robertson and Rossiter's studies only boys were interviewed. There is a need for more controlled and systematic research.

In virtually all of the existing research, the conclusions one reaches are based on the replies of children (and/or of their mothers, not fathers) to survey questions or, much more rarely, upon direct observation of the children's behavior. While the survey approach is certainly a useful one for determining perceptions of, attitudes toward and opinions of advertising, it does not tell us, except in indirect ways, about advertising's actual effects upon children.

Careful investigations of the ways in which children process televised messages are needed, including studies of their perception, comprehension and recall of both the secondary and central aspects of the commercials. This research could provide a set of general principles that would allow advertisers to anticipate to a degree which messages might have undesirable or desirable effects.

Children can learn concepts from television shows and commercials, and they can translate what they learn into action. While children certainly understand commercials—in that children remember brand names, identify brands in stores, remember dialogue used in the commercial, know what the product does, and ask their parents for it in the store—this very responsiveness of young children to advertising shows the beginnings of consumer learning behavior and imposes special obligations upon advertisers to be aware of the influence and effects of their advertisements on children.

Balance Theory and the Job vs College Decision
by Kathleen S. Burton

According to Rosenberg and Abelson's (1960) model on attitude change, if a person's attitudes of two objects and the relationship between them are inconsistent, that person will be in a state of imbalance. In order to come to a decision, he/she will have to change his/her attitude toward one or more of the objects or their relationship in order to come to a state of equilibrium. This theory can be illustrated in the example of a person who is trying to decide whether or not to quit a job and go back to college on a full time basis. The graph for the original situation is:

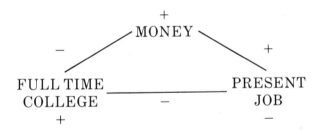

The person in question positively values money earned. He/she is not satisfied with his/her present job, and he/she likes the idea of going back to college on a full time basis in order to obtain a degree. However, the person's present job is positively associated with earning money. Going back to college full time means that the person won't be able to earn the money he/she is able to presently. In order to go back to school full time, he/she will have to quit this present job.

There are two inconsistencies in this situation which the individual needs to change in order to come to equilibrium. The first is between the person's attitudes towards money and his/her present job. The second is between his/her attitudes towards money and full time college.

One possible change that the individual can make is in his/her attitude toward money. If he/she decides that earning money is too capitalistic a value, the situation will be in equilibrium and the graph will change to the following:

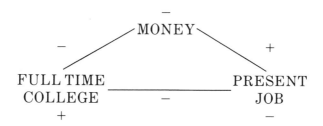

If the person highly values earning money, this change may not be a possibility. But Rosenberg and Abelson do not consider in their model the degree to which a person holds an attitude.

A second possibility would be to change the values he/she places on going back to college and on his/her present job. The individual might decide that going back to college on a full time basis wouldn't really help him or her that much and that studying takes too much time. In this situation he/she will also have to decide that he/she really does like the present job. Perhaps the individual has reconsidered the idea of leaving his/her friends at work or dislikes the idea of giving up the seniority built up in this job. These two changes might be particularly applicable at a time when there is a tight labor market with few available jobs and high unemployment rates. The graph showing this change is:

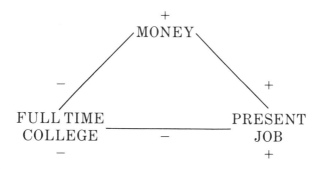

A third possible solution would involve the changing of perceptions of two relationships between objects. The person could first change his/her peception of the relationship between earned money and the present job. Perhaps he/she really is not earning enough money to comfortably support him/herself. In that case, these two objects will be negatively associated. The individual would also have to change his/her perception of the relationship between money and going back to college full time. In this instance he/she would have to believe that going back to college to obtain a degree would mean that in the future, his/her earnings would be enough to make up for the earnings lost while completing his/her education. These changes will also bring the situation to a state of equilibrium.

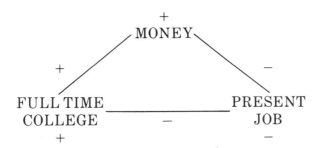

As stated previously, Rosenberg and Abelson do not account for the degree to which a person holds an attitude. The theory tends to look at the overall attitudes toward objects such as going back to college full time and the person's present job. There are many dimensions involved in each of these objects which, in themselves, could cause inconsistencies in the individual's attitude. In the person's present job he/she may be unhappy with the pay and fringe benefits but the individual may like the people he/she works with and the seniority he/she has attained. In going back to college the person may like the idea of becoming more educated and of meeting new people, but may dislike the thought of spending weekends cramming for exams. Each of these factors could be divided into other dimensions. So the attitudes toward objects do have to be generalized at some point to make this model work.

Although Rosenberg and Abelson's model gives several alternatives for attitude changes in a given situation, it does not attempt to predict which alternative a particular person will choose among those involving equal numbers of changes. That depends on how strongly the individual feels about the different elements in each option.

Cognitive Dissonance and the Pet Purchase
by Debra Joy Bargeski

One factor which influences a buyer's choice of a pet is that of cognitive dissonance. The theory of cognitive dissonance can best be explained by defining the two terms of its title. A cognition may be defined as "any knowledge, opinion, or belief about the environment, about one's self, or about one's behavior" (Runyon 1977). Any two cognitions are said to be dissonant when there are appasent inconsistencies, thus causing psychological tension within the individual.

The existence of cognitive dissonance is the natural result of making a purchasing decision. There would be no real decision at hand if all the features in the cognition of one alternative, taken by itself, favored its selection while all the features of the other alternative, taken by itself, would result in its rejection. Thus, following a decision, the purchaser is confronted with the dissonant cognitions that the rejected alternative had attractive features but that these features can no longer be enjoyed.

As viewed by dissonance theory, the purchasing decision, as associated with the pet market, would be something like this. Confronted with the necessity of choosing between alternatives, whether they be that of buying through a professional breeder or that of buying from a pet shop, or even choosing between two different breeds, the buyer would begin collecting and evaluating information about these alternatives, eventually establishing a preference order. This does not have to result in a decision because the process continues until the decision-maker has adequate confidence to act. Once the required confidence level has been reached it is assumed that the buyer will choose the most favorable alternative.

After the decision has been made, dissonance and the strain to reduce it begin to exert their influence. If the buyer's present experience with the pet is satisfactory, the decrease of post-choice dissonance should increase his/her preference for the type of pet he/she just bought. The degree to which this attitude change would occur depends upon the extent of the dissonance. For example, if buyers are accustomed to purchasing their pets through a private breeder, they would experience a high dissonance from purchasing a pet by way of a pet shop, if they've been pleased with the results of purchasing through private households and as such may undergo considerable change of attitude toward pet shops.

To aid the individual in reducing the discomfort due to dissonance, several of the following methods may be of assistance. The purchaser may return the pet, thereby rescinding his/her previous decision. Some public pet shops have a stiff return policy in which the consumer must purchase another pet of the identical value within a 90-day period, or he/she waves his/her warranty privileges. However, many private breeders allow for "terms." If the pet is found to have an illness stemming from its birth, the terms most probably would be an exchange of the pet for one available at present or for one available in the future, or a return of the purchaser's payment.

Another method of reducing dissonance would be for the individual to collect and evaluate additional favorable information about the place of purchase or the pet itself. Either through word-of-mouth, or by contacting the Better Business Bureau, one can find out about the public pet shops. In order to check on the background of the private breeder, one may consult the local veterinarian, local dog clubs and associations, other breeders or past customers, or the American Kennel Club. The final suggestion for reducing dissonance is that the individual may emphasize the positive features of the purchase and emphasize the negative features of the alternative selection. This can be accomplished by use and comparison of the information collected. One may focus on the cost differential, guarantee and warranty policies, or credit terms available. Private households may offer a fairer and more realistic price than public businesses, or vice versa. Also, guarantees and warranties, as well as credit terms, may be adjusted to the individual customer when one deals with private breeders. Some public pet shops do not vary their terms accordingly. They have one return policy, and their installment plan is set up according to the price of the pet, not according to the individual's financial circumstances.

"Post purchase dissonance" is most likely to result when:

(1) the decision is important in terms of financial expenditures or the psychological significance to the individual consumer. One interested in showing the pet in obedience or conformation will be more open to spending a greater amount of money for a higher quality animal. However, if one is only concerned with a "pet," then one is less willing to spend a lot of money.

(2) a variety of desirable alternatives is available. These alternatives include private vs public, pet vs show, male vs female, etc.

(3) the alternatives, while rated similarly, are qualitatively dissimilar and there is little "cognitive overlap" or shared features. Therefore a decision between a horse and a dog creates a higher degree of dissonance than a decision between a Golden Retriever and an Irish Setter.

(4) the consumer's decision is the result of free will, with little or no outside applied pressure. However, if pressure should be applied, the purchaser complies without allowing his/her cognitions to be disputed. The individual may experience outside pressures from his/her peer group, from breeders, professional handlers, judges, veterinarians, and pet shop owners and employees.

REFERENCES

ANON. 1970. Television and Growing-up: The Impact of Televised Violence. Report to the Surgeon General from the Scientific Advisory Committee on Television and Social Behavior. U.S. Govnt. Printing Off., Washington, D.C.

ARONSON, E. and MILLS, J. 1959. The effect of severity of initiation on liking for a group. J. Abnormal Soc. Psychol. 59, 177-181.

BANDURA, A. and WALTERS, R. H. 1963. Social Learning and Personality Development. Holt, Rinehart, and Winston, New York.

BEM, D. 1967. Self-perception: An alternative interpretation of cognitive dissonance phenomena. Psychol. Rev. 74, 183-200.

BLISS, P. 1967. Marketing and the Behavioral Sciences. Allyn and Bascon, Boston.

CALDER, B. 1973. Cognitive consistency and consumer behavior. In Perspectives in Consumer Behavior (rev. ed.) (H. Kassarjian and T. Robertson, Editors.) Scott, Foresman and Co., Glenview, Illinois.

DOLLARD, J. and MILLER, N. 1950. Personality and Psychotherapy. McGraw-Hill, New York.

EFRON, E. and HICKEY, N. 1969. Television and your child. T.V. Guide Magazine.

EHRLICH, D. et. al. 1957. Post-decision exposure to relevant information. J. Abnormal Soc. Psychol. 54, 98-102.

FESTINGER, L. and CARLSMITH, J. 1959. Cognitive consequences of forced compliance. J. Abnormal Soc. Psychol. 58, 203-210.

FOWLES, B. and VOYAT, G. 1974. Piaget meets big bird: Is T.V. a passive teacher? Urban Rev. 7 (1) 69-80.

GERBNER, C. 1974. Television image in mass culture. In Media and Symbols. D. Olson (Editor.) Univ. of Chicago Press, Chicago.

GOLDBERG, M. and GORN, G. 1974. Children's reactions to television advertising: An experimental approach. J. Consumer Res. 1 (2) 69-75.

HEIDER, F. 1946. Attitudes and cognitive organization. J. Psychol. 21, 107-112.

HELITZER, M. 1970. The Youth Market. Media Books, New York.

HILGARD, E. and BOWEN, G. 1966. Theories of Learning. Appleton-Century-Crofts, New York.

HILGARD, E. and BOWEN, G. 1975. Theories of Learning (4th ed.) Prentice-Hall, Englewood Cliffs, N.J.

HORTON, D. and TURNAGE, T. 1976. Human Learning. Prentice-Hall, Englewood Cliffs, N.J.

HULL, C. 1939. The problem of stimulus equivalence in behavior theory. Psychol. Rev. 46, 9-30.

JORDAN, N. 1953. Behavioral forces that are a function of attitudes and of cognitive organization. Human Relations 6, 273-287.

KASSARJIAN, H. and COHEN, J. 1965. Cognitive dissonance and consumer behavior. Calif. Manag. Rev. 8, 55-64.

KAYE, E. 1974. The Family Guide to Children's Television. Random House, New York.

KRUGMAN, H. E. 1962. An application of learning theory to T.V. copy testing. Publ. Opin. Quart. *26*, 626–634.

KRUGMAN, H. E. 1965. Impact of T.V. advertising: Learning without involvement. Publ. Opin. Quart. *29*, 349–356.

LESSER, G. S. 1974. Children and Television: Lessons From Sesame Street. Random House, New York.

MARKIN, R. J., Jr. 1974. Consumer Behavior: A Cognitive Orientation. MacMillan Publishing Co., New York.

MITTELSTAEDT, R. 1966. An experimental study of the effects of experience on consumer decision making. *In* Science, Technology and Marketing. (R. Hass, Editor.) American Marketing Association, Chicago.

MURRAY, J. 1973. Television and violence. Amer. Psychol. (June).

NEISSER, U. 1976. Cognition and Reality. W.H. Freeman and Co., San Francisco.

OSGOOD, C. and TANNENBAUM, P. 1955. The principle of congruity in the prediction of attitude change. Psychol. Rev. *62*, 42-55.

PALMER, E., GIBBON, S. and FOWLES, B. 1975. Sesame Street, the Electric Company, and reading. *In* Toward a Literate Society, J. B. Carroll (Ed.) Random House, New York.

PERVIN, L. 1975. Personality: Theory, Assessment and Research. John Wiley and Sons, New York.

PIAGET, J. 1970. Piaget's theory. *In* Carmichael's Manual of Child Psychology, Vol. 1. P. Mussen (Ed.) John Wiley and Sons, New York.

POULOS, R. W. 1976. Unintentional negative side effects of food commercials. Broadcast Advert. and Children. U.S. Printing Office, Washington, D.C.

ROBERTSON, T. and ROSSITER, J. 1974. Children and commercial persuasion: An attribution theory analysis. J. Consumer Res. *1* (1) 13–20.

ROBERTSON, T. and ROSSITER, J. 1974. Children's T.V. commercials, testing the defenses. J. Comm. *24* (4) 137–144.

ROSENBERG, M., HOVLAND, C., McGUIRE, W., ABELSON, R. and BREHM, J. 1960. Attitude Organization and Change. Yale Univ. Press, New Haven.

RUNYON, K. E. 1977. Consumer Behavior and the Practice of Marketing. Charles E. Merrill Publishing Co., Columbus, Ohio.

SHERIF, C., SHERIF, M. and NEBERGALL, R. 1965. Attitude and Attitude Change: The Social Judgment-involvement Approach. W.B. Saunders Company, Philadelphia.

SKINNER, B. 1953. Science and Human Behavior. MacMillan, New York.

THORNDIKE, E. 1913. The Psychology of Learning. Teachers College, New York.

THORNDIKE, E. 1932. The Fundamentals of Learning. Teachers College, New York.

WARD, S. 1972. Children's reactions to commercials. J. Advert. Res. 12, 37–44.

WELLS, W. 1965. Communicating with children. J. Advert. Res. 5 (2) 2–14.

ZAJONC, R. 1960. The concepts of balance, congruity and dissonance. Public Opinion Quart. 24, 280-296.

8

Exchange Theory in Economics and Social Psychology

Exchange theory has been developed more or less independently in economics and social psychology. Surprisingly enough,
considering this independence, the results from both seem to
converge to a single framework, complementing each other.
Economic theory has provided the framework of the analysis
and social psychology has investigated the portion which is indeterminate (or only partially determinate) in economic theory.

THE ECONOMIC FRAMEWORK

The same indifference curve analysis as described previously
applies here. For simplicity, the elements on the axes will be
referred to as "goods," although as previously discussed they
need not be physical goods. Assume two people and between
them a fixed amount of each of the two goods, X and Y. Each
individual will have an indifference map as previously described.
As the resources are fixed, the graph of one individual can be
rotated 180° and superimposed on the other (Fig. 8.1). There is
only so much of good X between the two people; what one person
does not have the other has.

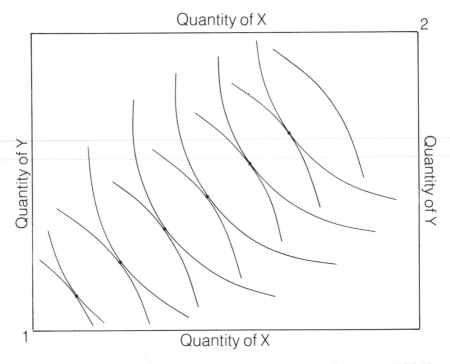

FIG. 8.1.   INDIFFERENCE CURVES OF TWO INDIVIDUALS SUPERIMPOSED

Where the individual's indifference curves are tangent, neither can be made better off except at the expense of the other. As seen in Fig. 8.1, at such points person 1 can not move northeast to a higher indifference curve without pushing person 2 down to a lower indifference curve. Moving northeast on the diagram means less satisfaction for person 2. As neither individual will allow him/herself to be made worse off through trading, trade in these situations is impossible.

The individuals will have an initial allocation of the two goods. Only when at this initial allocation their indifference curves intersect will trade be possible (Fig. 8.2). With this intersection both parties can reach higher indifference curves through trade. If person 1 will be made worse off by trade than he/she was already, person 1 will simply refuse to trade. As person 1 will refuse to go southwest of C^1 in trade, and person 2 will refuse to go northeast of C^2, the trading area is between C^1 and C^2. Therefore, only a section of the total indifference map becomes relevant for the trade (Fig. 8.3). As C^1 and C^2 represent how

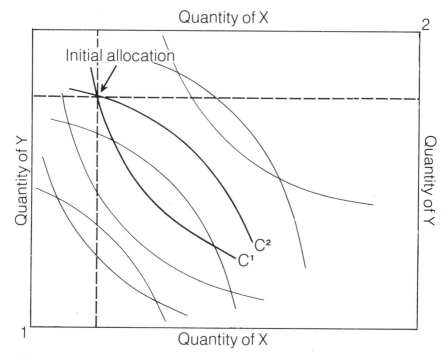

FIG. 8.2. INITIAL ALLOCATION OF TWO GOODS BY TWO INDIVIDUALS

well off the person initially is and the level of satisfaction which any alternative to the present position would have to provide in order to be considered, C^1 and C^2 can be thought of as the comparison levels for alternatives for persons 1 and 2, to use Thibaut and Kelley's (1959) terminology.

Since where the individuals indifference curves are tangent neither can be made better off except at the expense of the other. These points are the efficient trades. Graphically, the locus of these points is known as the "contract curve" (Fig. 8.4). The exchange ratio between the two goods, analogous to the comparison level of the trade discussed later, is determined by the trade and is represented by a line from the initial allocation through the contract curve at the trade (Fig. 8.5).

Where on the contract curve the two traders end up is indeterminate in a pure barter situation. Noneconomic and sociopsychological factors are involved.

If prices already exist and neither trader may influence the price, each trader operates along an "offer curve," which is the

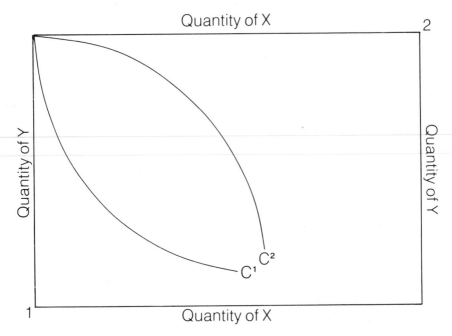

FIG. 8.3.   RELEVANT INDIFFERENCE CURVES FOR TRADE BY TWO
INDIVIDUALS

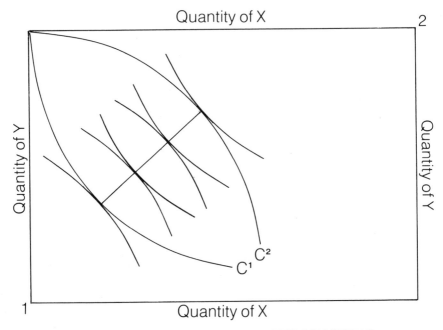

FIG. 8.4.   THE CONTRACT CURVE BETWEEN TWO INDIVIDUALS

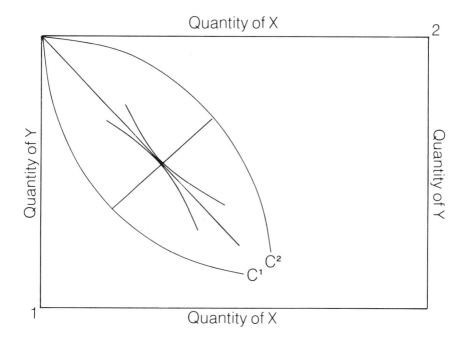

FIG. 8.5.   EXCHANGE RATIO BETWEEN TWO GOODS BY TWO
INDIVIDUALS

locus of the tangencies of various price ratios to higher indifference curves (Fig. 8.6). In this case, the intersection of the two
offer curves determines the trading result (Fig. 8.7), as this is
the only point at which both parties maximize their utility with
respect to the budget constraints. At this point, both individuals' indifference curves are tangent to each other and to the
exchange ratio line. A slight rearrangement of the graph yields
Fig. 8.8. Here no bargaining occurs. There exists only a mutual
exchange of information to determine the trading point. This
situation is not very realistic except possibly in agriculture and
international trade, almost certainly not in two-person relationships.

   The acquisition of market power by one party over the other,
that is, one party realizes his/her ability to influence the terms of
trade, reduces but does not eliminate the indeterminancy of the
barter situation. If the other party cannot influence price, he/
she will operate along his/her offer curve. The powerful party 1

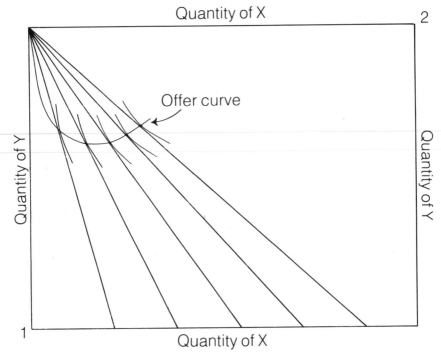

FIG. 8.6.   OFFER CURVE IN A BARTER SITUATION

will choose the price so the offer curve of party 2 is tangent to the highest possible indifference curve of party 1. Party 1, therefore, will maximize his/her utility subject to operations by party 2 (Fig. 8.9).

This point does not lie on the contract curve; it is not efficient, so further incentive exists to trade. Another indeterminate segment of the contract curve, smaller than the original indeterminate region, becomes evident. The parties then begin all over again in the process described above. The person with the greater power is thus able to push the other toward his/her (the other's) initial allocation indifference curve and corresponding end of the contract curve. If party 2 never reacts to the power situation by abandoning his/her offer curve, the process converges to a point on the contract curve very much in favor of party 1, as in a monopoly situation. If one relaxes this assumption on party 2, however slightly, the whole result becomes indeterminate again.

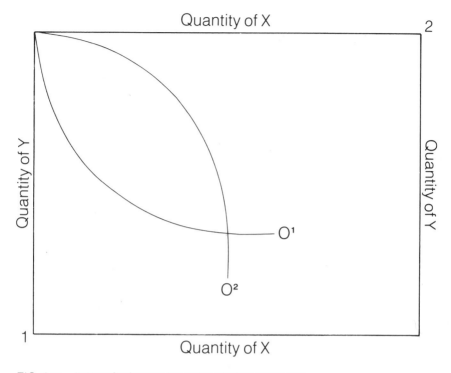

FIG. 8.7.   INTERSECTION OF TWO OFFER CURVES

SOCIAL PSYCHOLOGICAL INTERPRETATIONS

This analysis can easily be interpreted in the context of Thibaut and Kelley's (1959) social psychological exchange theory. The indifference curves corresponding to the initial allocation are the comparison levels for alternatives (CLALT) of Thibaut and Kelley, while the exchange ratio is the comparison level for this trade (CL) to the individual. The lower the comparison level/exchange ratio for one individual, the higher it becomes for the other. This measures relative gains along the contract curve. If the exchange ratio is below the initial-allocation indifference curve (the CL below the CLALT), the individual simply will not trade, as he/she would be made worse off. The higher the CL, the better off that individual is, i.e., the more the exchange line swings away from an individual's initial-allocation indifference curve, the better he/she does by trading.

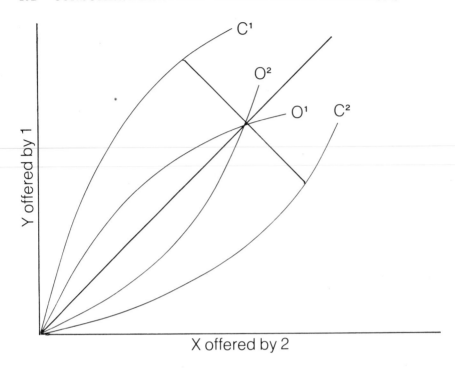

FIG. 8.8.   TRADING POINT BY TWO INDIVIDUALS

Thibaut and Kelley listed possible strategies for person A to increase his/her power over person B in the two-person situation: (1) develop better alternatives for A, raising his/her CL_{ALT} so B's performance would keep him/her barely above it, (2) reduce B's alternatives, (3) improve A's ability to reward B, (4) reduce B's skills, (5) build up the value of A's product, (6) devalue B's product, and (7) lengthen A's time perspective (defer rewards to future, lowering A's dependence on B).

For example, consider an employer (person A) and employee (person B). The employer will have more power over the employee if the employer has an alternative supply of capable potential workers; the employee then must perform better to maintain his/her job. The employer may be able to change the employee's alternatives through blacklisting or unfavorable recommendation. The employer may also make his/her plant a more attractive place to work, through better working conditions, increasing the value of the employer's product to offer the employee, or through increased prosperity which would in-

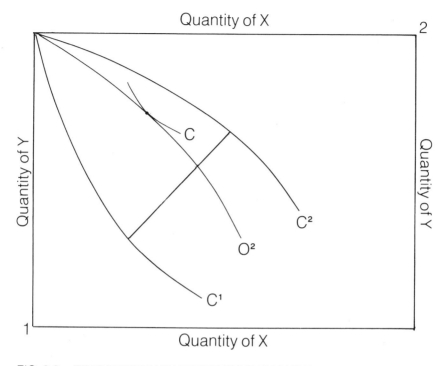

Quantity of X

FIG. 8.9.   TRADING WITH MARKET POWER BY ONE PARTY

crease the employer's ability to reward the employee. The employer may reduce the employee's skills by assigning him/her to jobs for which he/she is unsuited; the employer may devalue the employee's product by simply considering the work the employee does as less important than before. If the employer has a task which must be completed immediately, the employee may well be the only one available who can do it. If the employer can wait longer, he/she may find other workers with this ability and as such will be less dependent on and have more power over this one employee. The exchange is of the employee's labor for the employer's money and/or other benefits. The more power the employer acquires in this situation, the more favorable to the employer any contract will be. This can easily be reflected in the graphs just described.

Blau (1964) deals with four requirements of power; the person must (1) remain indifferent to benefits others can offer in exchange for his/hers, (2) bar access to alternative suppliers of services the person has, (3) prevent others from using coercive force as in coalitions to effect their demands, and (4) maintain others' needs for a person's services. These are similar to but not identical with Thibaut and Kelley's strategies. Both lists deal mainly with ways for the person to become less dependent on the other party. These can be interpreted with respect to both economic dependence and emotional dependence. The less dependent person has the greater power in the situation and is thus in the better position to exact demands from the other. The person who cares most or has the greatest need occupies the weakest position in the relationship.

Homans (1961) supports the analogy of general economic principles with social psychology. For example, his proposition that the more often a person has received a reward from another the less valuable any further unit of reward becomes to him or her, simply restates the idea of a diminishing marginal rate of substitution. Under marginal utility theory, diminishing marginal utility would have applied. Homans' concepts of cost and profit are also the economic opportunity cost and profit. Blau (1964),

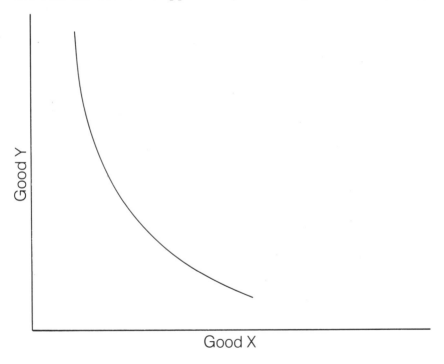

FIG. 8.10.   AN INDIVIDUAL VALUES GOOD X RELATIVELY HIGHER THAN Y

who derives most of his analysis in the respect from Homans, is more specific about costs, identifying time as the major factor in psychological relationships.

Homans also correctly broadens the concept of price to mean reward and/or cost, as in the laws of supply and demand. Economics has confined its activity mostly to monetary price simply because it is easiest to measure; the entire previous argument has held that this need not be so. Blau (1964) goes into greater detail on the psychic factors involved.

While several of Homans' assertions concerning economic assumptions are incorrect, his proposition that the tougher bargainer values less highly the reward the other can offer is consistent with indifference curves in the exchange analysis presented previously. In Fig. 8.10, the person values good X more highly than in Fig. 8.11, as it requires more Y to reconcile him/her with a unit loss of good X than it does in Fig. 8.11. This also affects the shape of the initial indifference curves (Fig. 8.12), and thus alters the bargaining region in person 1's favor

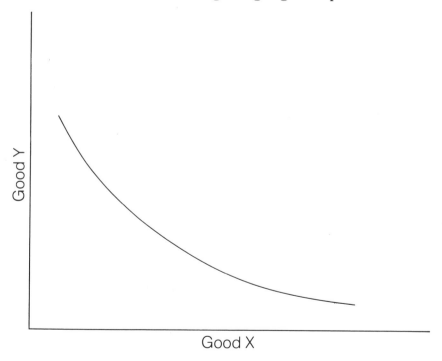

FIG. 8.11.   AN INDIVIDUAL VALUES GOOD Y RELATIVELY HIGHER THAN X

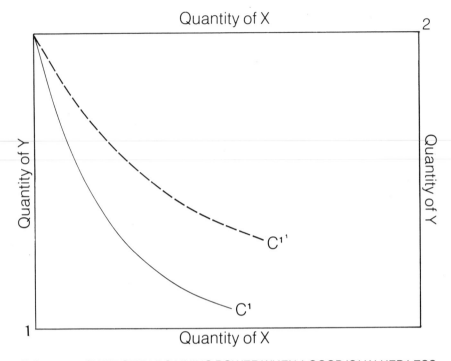

FIG. 8.12.   SHIFT OF BARGAINING POWER WHEN A GOOD IS VALUED LESS HIGHLY

when he/she values less highly the other's good. In the case of offer curves, this lesser dependence through shifting of indifference curves shifts the offer curve, which alters the terms of trade thus determined (Fig. 8.13). Thibaut and Kelley (1959) expressed the same idea in terms of comparison levels for the relationship and for alternatives. This again emphasizes the importance of relative dependence, which is the key to relative power in the negotiating relationship.

TOUGHNESS IN BARGAINING

If one assumes the pure barter case, the indeterminancy along the contract curve can be determined, at least in part, by which partner is the tougher bargainer. Social psychological research has explored some of the factors influencing toughness in bargaining, generally under the barter situation.

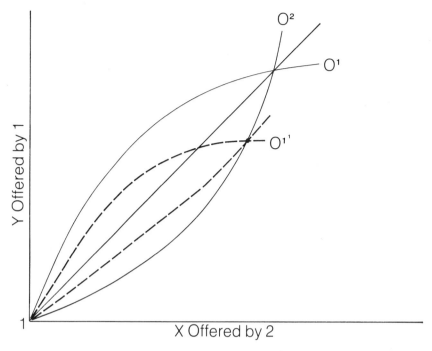

FIG. 8.13.   OFFER CURVE SHIFTED WITH LESSER DEPENDENCE BY 1

Information

Bartos (1970) held that information is a key element in bargaining; negotiation and the give and take of offers and counteroffers will not occur unless each participant is at least partially ignorant of his/her opponent's true interests. Otherwise, they could reach an agreement immediately. Kelley and Thibaut (1969) stress that mutual informational dependence and possible control is more predominant than actual outcome control because it is more advantageous. Thus, a monopolistic party 1 would operate along party 2's offer curve by leading party 2 to believe that party 1 was also a competitive price taker, rather than by forcing the power structure and outcome on party 2.

Kahn and Kohls (1972) found that the less information relevant to the task the bargainers possess, the tougher will be the bargaining because both sides will be uncertain as to what is reasonable to expect and toughness is a safer and potentially more information-gathering approach. This has also been found by Kelley (1966); Kelly, Beckman and Fisher (1967); Liebert *et al.* (1968); and Siegel and Fouraker (1960).

Liebert *et al.* (1968) compared completely and incompletely informed subjects. The former knew the possible range of profits for both themselves and their opponents, and the latter knew it only for themselves. The hypothesis supported was that the uninformed use their opponents' bids to set their own goals, while the informed use them to assess the reasonableness of opponents' goals. For example, if a person selling a car has little information on what his/her car is worth or what the prospective buyer might pay elsewhere, the seller may set his/her expectations by the buyer's offer. If the seller knows the used car market fairly well, he/she will take the offer as an indication of their how realistic or honest the buyer is, rather than as an indication of what the car is worth.

Another form of information Kahn and Kohls (1972) found relevant was the bargainer's perception of his/her own toughness, as formed relative to a group in prenegotiation discussion. Toughness apparently carries a positive social value in terms of prestige and each bargainer thinks he/she is tough. In the group, he/she finds that since others are also tough, he/she must become tougher to keep his/her self-image. In this way and in effects on outcomes, toughness is very similar to risk-taking to which this explanation also applies. The "risky shift" of a group from the original positions of its members to a position of greater risk has long intrigued social psychologists.

Other Factors

Druckman (1968) found that a prebargaining atmosphere which leads to consideration of the debate as collaborative problem solving facilitates conflict resolution. In this situation, neither side is originally committed to a hard-line, unilateral position. This atmosphere may occur in bilateral open discussion before either side has a chance to develop a rationale for its own position. He also suggested (Druckman 1967) that the personalities of the individuals involved would have a relevant effect; specifically, more dogmatic personalities would be more resistant to compromise than would less dogmatic people.

Kelley, Beckman and Fisher (1967) found that high minimum requirements for the bargainers result in taking a longer time to negotiate, a characteristic of tough bargaining. If both parties enter negotiations with high minimum acceptable outcomes, a mutually acceptable solution will not be easy to accomplish. There is a resistance, R, to making further concessions; assumptions about R include (1) the higher R, the longer time required for further concessions to come forth, (2) the more likely for that party to quit negotiations, (3) the party with the lower R will make the next concession, (4) pressures of time and persuasion are equally effective for both parties, (5) for a given minimum requirement level, the R to each successive concession increases as the person moves toward that level. This assumption can be easily visualized on the contract curve; the initial indifference curves represent the minimum requirement levels. These assumptions are fully consistent with and supplementary to the economic framework above. A person will be increasingly more reluctant to make concessions as he/she approaches, from above, his/her indifference curve for the initial allocation. The assumptions are also similar to Harsanyi's (1956) findings.

Harsanyi (1956) in a review of Zeuthen's and Nash's findings, considered the risk of conflict each party is prepared to face in order to secure a more advantageous outcome. The person who is less prepared to face this risk of conflict will be more likely to make concessions in the bargaining situation. For example, in a family bargaining situation, the spouse who most highly values peace in the family is the most likely to give way in negotiations to the other, if it appears that his/her point can be won only through conflict. Risk-taking, thus, seems to be closely related to toughness, and may be a significant part of toughness.

Where on the contract curve the bargaining parties end up largely depends on relative power and toughness in the bargaining situation. The underlining theme indicates that the party which is less dependent on the other has the most advantageous position. Besides the ways listed by Thibaut and Kelley (1959) and Blau (1964) in which this independence could increase, information appears to be the major factor in determining relative power and the resulting contract point.

EXCHANGE WITHIN THE FAMILY

The exchange process can be readily applied to the family. Many purchase decisions are made as a household unit. The members of that unit, usually members of a family, must jointly make that decision or decide to allow one member to make the decision. This requires negotiation between the members since each person will likely have different preferences. Frequently, a person may allow another his/her decision on one matter in return for concessions on another. Again, one need not limit the analysis to tangible goods. For example, a husband may take his wife out to dinner in return for greater affection later.

We will consider a husband-wife family unit, since these members account for most family decisions. Males generally have the most power in a relationship, as documented by sociologists (Walum 1977). Analogies can be drawn from the determinants of and strategies for increasing power to the family situation. For example, females generally are more isolated from the rest of society and therefore have fewer alternatives than do males. The implication for present purposes is that the person with the most power will have the most influence on the family or group decision. This decision then will largely reflect the preferences of that person.

Husbands do make more decisions and more problem-solving actions than their wives, who specialize in social and emotional support (Kenkel 1957). The extent to which this takes place depends on personality variables of dominance and self-confidence. As the above division of labor becomes stronger, the more dominant and less self-confident the husband becomes (Kenkel 1961B). Apparently, the more self-confident partners feel freer to depart from traditional sex roles. This directly affects the result of the family decision (Kenkel 1961A).

The amount of information the husband and wife have in making a decision affects their relative roles in the decision (Gardner 1971). With little information, the wife takes an active part in the problem-solving aspect; as the amount of information increases, she leaves the decision to her husband and becomes a more passive, supportive partner. Although one should not infer that marriage is primarily a combat zone, the more active role of the wife under little information concurs with the relationship of little information to toughness in bargaining advanced by Kahn and Kohls (1972).

The pattern of influence in making decisions varies with age, income class, role perception and type of purchase (Green and Cunningham 1975). More joint decisions are made among younger couples and in the middle-income classes. Women with liberal perceptions of the female role make more decisions or have a greater share in decisions than do women with more traditional orientations. This difference is greater among younger, upper- and middle-income couples and for major appliances, cars and vacations. As the status and autonomy of the wife increases, she makes more decisions. Again, this is consistent with the exchange theory implications. This in turn will affect the pattern of consumption.

The length of the marriage and the stage in the family life cycle also affects the decision pattern (Cox 1975). In the early years of marriage, more joint decisions take place on long-range plans. Negotiation and compromise are needed. The exchange model with its emphasis on bargaining is most appropriate here. As the length of marriage increases and as children arrive, the preferences of husband and wife become more similar so less need exists for negotiation. A norm has been established and the partners are apt to make independent decisions using this norm as reference. Cox suggests that in these years the family could better be considered as a small group. The literature on group influence then applies.

Thus, the basic framework for exchange analysis has been developed in economic theory. Social psychology has, perhaps unconsciously, been operating within this framework to examine the psychological factors of why a contract will take place where it does on the contract curve, in the traditional barter situation. Relative dependence, in which information is involved, seems to be the key. Economic theory by itself does not answer the question except in special cases or in general limitations on possibilities. If the factors involved could be quantified, more accurate predictions could be made.

APPLICATION OF THEORIES

Family Buying Decision-making
by Doris Cunningham

The purpose of this report is to examine two major determinants of family purchasing decisions.

One determinant of family purchasing behavior is the impact which changes in the female role have upon family purchasing behavior. Sex roles have undergone major changes in the last 15 years and have influenced the nature of marriage as well as occupational choices. Traditionally, the husband has made most of the major family decisions and so these decisions largely reflect the husbands' preferences. One would expect less husband decision-making in families where the wife holds contemporary attitudes toward the female role.

A second determinant is the family life cycle and in particular the presence of children; it is this, rather than the length of marriage which brings about goal-congruent behavior through similarity of preferences between husband and wife.

Neither of these determinants discussed in this paper are expected to be purely American phenomena.

Feminine Role Perception and Family Purchasing Decisions. — The objective of a study by Robert T. Green and Isabella C.M. Cunningham (1975) is to examine differences that exist in consumption-related aspects of family decison-making between families in which the wife is characterized by varying attitudes toward the woman's role. The potential impact which changes in the female role will have upon family purchasing patterns is studied.

Findings in the past have indicated sex role differences in decision-making with respect to many products. It has been assumed that the husband makes decisions about life insurance and automobiles. Decisions about some products such as groceries tend to be the domain of the wife. Joint husband-wife decisions are housing and vacations. In general the husband has been found to be the more dominant decision-maker concerning instrumental purchase decisions.

Family purchasing roles tend to vary between different income classes. The upper and lower-income classes are characterized by greater husband-wife autonomy in decision-making than the middle-income classes. Family purchasing patterns also tend to vary with the age of the couple. Komorovsky (1961) points out the existence of more joint decision-making among younger couples. Sharp and Mott (1956) point out more wife participation in life insurance decisions among older couples.

Sex role changes occurring in society will produce changes in family purchasing roles. Since the husband has traditionally been the dominant economic decision-maker in the family, then families with more contemporary role orientation should be characterized by less husband autonomy in purchasing decisions. Many purchasing decisions which are made primarily by the husband in traditional families will be joint husband-wife decisions in families with more contemporary role orientation. The increased status and autonomy of the modern wife implies that she will make some of the decisions previously made by the husband. Across all categories the power of the husband in family purchasing decisions has declined.

Method.—The method used in the Green-Cunningham study consisted of 250 randomly selected married women from Texas who completed a self-administered questionnaire. The respondents were presented with a list of 10 products and services together with a number of specific decisions that have to be made when purchasing each product and service. They were asked whether each decision was usually made by the wife, the husband or both the husband and wife. The respondents were presented with an inventory of attitudes associated with the female role. Demographic data were collected. In the products and services test respondents were asked to identify the primary decision-maker involved in 38 separate decisions.

The extent to which the respondents held contemporary attitudes with regard to the female role was indicated by their responses to the Autonomy Inventory, a 10-item Likert type scale developed by Arnott. The items employed in the Autonomy Inventory measure the extent of agreement with statements concerning aspects of the woman's role in society which would separate women who hold traditional concepts of their role from those who possess more contemporary attitudes.

On the basis of their Autonomy Inventory scores, the respondents were divided into three groups: conservatives, moderates and liberals. Conservatives hold attitudes identified with the traditional role of women. Liberals are women who have contemporary attitudes toward the female role. Moderates represented an intermediate group, whose role perceptions either vacillated on the items, or whose attitudes toward the various aspects of the female role represented in the scale are not strongly held.

Analysis.—The number of "husband usually," "both husband and wife" and "wife usually" decisions were summed for each product and service across all products and services. Significant differences between the three groups of women would suggest that conservatives, moderates and liberals tend to play different roles in family purchasing decisions.

Previous literature states that women tend to make decisions which relate to the expressive aspects of a product, while men tend to make such instrumental decisions as the amount to spend on an item. Chi-square analysis was used to test for differences between conservatives, moderates and liberals on the number of husband, wife and joint decisions made concerning the amount to spend on each of the eight products and services and across the eight products and services. The previous literature indicates that husband-wife purchasing roles tend to differ between age groups and income groups.

Research Findings.—The results with respect to the total number of husband, joint and wife decisions made by the groups indicate that the husbands of liberal wives tend to make fewer buying decisions than husbands of conservative and moderate women. Decisions related to groceries are wife dominated for liberals, moderates and conservatives, while life insurance decisions are husband-dominated in the three groups. Furniture is jointly decided regardless of attitude towards the woman's role. Decisions on family savings are split between joint and husband decisions across the groups. Housing decisions tend to be jointly made in all three groups.

The products which provide the greatest contribution to the total differences between the groups are major appliances, automobiles and vacations. In each of these areas, husbands of liberal wives were reported to make fewer decisions than husbands of conservative and moderate wives. Automobiles are characterized by significantly more joint decisions among liberals.

Decisions concerning the selection of the family doctor and money and bills show tendencies different from the total results. The former is characterized by more wife decision-making among liberals while the latter show less joint decision-making in the liberal group.

How Much to Spend.—The chi-square test was run on the total number of "how much to spend" decisions made by husbands, wives or jointly between conservatives, moderates and liberals. The proportional representation of conservatives, moderates and liberals in the cells shows that the major differences between the groups are in the husband and wife categories. Liberals show less husband and more wife decisions than moderates and conservatives. Significant differences are found between conservatives, moderates and liberals in the responses to questions concerning who decides how much to spend on furniture. Differences are not found between the three groups in response to similar questions concerning groceries, major appliances, life insurance and vacations. While overall differences exist between conservatives, moderates and liberals, along this dimension of decision-making, these differences seem to be caused by the decisions pertaining to particular products and services.

Purchase Decisions Within Income Categories.—The findings indicate significantly less husband decision-making among upper-income ($20,000–up) liberals. The specific product and service results show significant decision-making differences between upper-income conservatives, moderates and liberals on seven of the 10 items. With respect to major appliances, family savings, vacations and housing, the liberals exhibit significantly less husband decision-making than other groups. For life insurance and automobiles, the liberals are characterized by less husband and more joint decision-making than conservatives and moderates. Liberals report less joint and more wife decisions for grocery products.

The middle-income ($10,000–19,999) liberals exhibit significantly more wife decisions than the other groups. The individual products and services for which differences are found in the middle-income category consist of major appliances, automobiles and family doctor. In each case liberal wives make significantly more decisions than conservative and moderate wives. Liberals indicate less husband decisions for automobiles and less joint decisions for the family doctor.

The findings for lower income (less than $10,000) show no differences in total number of husband, joint and wife decisions between liberals, moderates and conservatives in the lower-income class. No significant decision-making differences are found between the three groups with respect to the individual products and services.

Purchase Decisions Within Age Categories.—Liberals in the younger age category (less than 35 years old) report significantly less husband decision-making than moderates and conservatives. The findings with respect to the individual product and services indicate significant differences in seven of the 10 items. Husbands of liberals are shown to make fewer decisions for furniture, major appliances, automobiles and family doctor than husbands of moderates and conservatives. With regard to vacations, liberals in the younger-age category exhibit less husband and more wife decisions. Both liberals and moderates depict their husbands as making fewer grocery and vacation decisions than conservatives.

In the 35 to 49 age category, liberals indicate significantly fewer husband decisions and more wife decisions than moderates and conservatives. Differences are found on four of the 10 products and services. Liberal wives tend to make more decisions for major appliances and family savings. Husbands make fewer vacation decisions in the liberal group.

In the 50 year old and above category no significant differences in the total number of husband, joint and wife decisions between the three subject groups were shown.

Discussion.—The use of only wives as the respondents in family decision-making studies has been the subject of much debate. Husbands' and wives' perceptions of decision-making authority in the family have not always been perfectly congruent. A second limitation involved the possibility that decisions concerning the products and services used in the study had not been made in the recent past. A portion of the sample was probably responding hypothetically to some of the products and services rather than on the basis of recent experience.

The findings provide a basis for speculation concerning the types of changes in purchasing behavior within the family which may be associated with the changes occuring in the female role. The hypothesis concerning less husband decision-making in families where the wife is characterized by contemporary attitudes toward the female role was confirmed by the results of the study. Husbands of liberal wives were perceived as making fewer purchase decisions on their own than was the case of husbands of either moderate or conservative wives. However, the data also indicated that this pattern may be product specific rather than generalized across all product categories. The liberal wives in the sample were reported to play a significantly greater role in deciding the amount of money to spend on purchases than moderate or conservative wives, although the findings also pertained to some products and services more than others.

The findings with respect to conservatives, moderates and liberals within different age and income categories suggests that the changes in buying behavior associated with the emerging female role may vary considerably among the sub-groups of society. In general the findings imply that the changes in purchase decision-making one would expect to associate with the changes in the female role may be more pervasive among liberals in the upper-income and in the younger-age groups.

The apparent purchasing role differences which were found in the younger-age and upper-income liberal groups may be tentatively explained by factors which characterize these groups. To the extent that higher incomes can be associated with greater general flexibility, families in the upper-income group may be more capable of making the adjustments for wife roles which correspond with the contemporary view of the female role. With regard to age, it can be postulated that husband-wife roles are not as well established in younger families and are easier to change.

The findings also suggest that marketers should exercise caution in assuming that women who hold contemporary attitudes of the female role are liberated or nontraditional in their purchase decision-making. The results indicate that not all women who possess these attributes are necessarily more autonomous in their buying decisions and that such attitudes may have a more pronounced impact on some products than others.

Family Purchase Decision-making and the Process of Adjustment.—Eli P. Cox III (1975) says research from social psychology, sociology and marketing suggests the importance of the process of adjustment in family purchase decision-making. Further empirical support is provided by a cross-sectional study which also indicates the superiority of family life cycles over length of marriage as an independent variable.

The belief that the family is a small group or is prototypical of the small group is fundamental to the family decision-making research. As with any social group, the family must have some degree of consensus regarding its goals, objectives and mode of operation if it is to exist and operate efficiently. These goals, objectives and modes of operation constitute part of the family's value hierarchy. The top of the hierarchy represents the most fundamental and intangible values. The lower levels of the hierarchy represent the more mundane values and attitudes. It appears that the position or importance of any particular value for the individual husband or wife as he or she views the family hierarchy would be dependent upon two things: (1) the position of the value in the individual's own personal hierarchy, and (2) the degree to which the individual perceived the value to be relevant to his or her family.

Early Marriage.—Early marriage is where intensive negotiation takes place regarding the shared family value hierarchy. Long-range plans are discussed regarding modes of raising children, career plans and major purchases such as house, furniture and automobile. There is a great deal of both joint decision-making and joint purchase activity in which special preferences and skills are revealed. In many areas husbands and wives may not agree upon the preferred alternative in the decision-making process. A compromise is necessary if any decision is to be made. These compromise decisions are important because they establish the precedent upon which the family will operate in the future.

Later Marriage.—After the initial state of flux in the marriage the family begins to operate from the basis of consensus and the compromise decisions of the past. Individual roles tend to become highly stabilized and joint decision-making and purchase activity is replaced by specialization of labor. As the marriage progresses, these compromise decisions are replaced by consensus decisions. The perceptions and preferences of husbands and wives involving items purchased by the family become more similar. This process of adjustment is probably the result of several forces. The family is a reference group. The husband and wife share membership in other reference groups and move toward views held by those groups. The family shares all the same information sources.

Method.—A cross-sectional study was conducted using questionnaire data from 93 married couples. These respondents were solicited through church, social and civic organizations in a medium-sized midwestern town. The respondents were slightly above the national average in terms of income, family size and percentage of wives who were employed.

To examine the process of adjustment, it was hypothesized that the preferences of husbands and wives for automobiles would be more similar for couples who had been married longer. Family life cycle was also examined as an independent variable which might prove to be more satisfactory than length of marriage in explaining the process of adjustment.

The husband and wife were asked separately to rank order a set of 10 automobiles upon the basis of their preference for them as realistic alternatives for a family car. Rank-order correlation was then calculated between these two lists of preference rank-ings and used as a measure of the degree of adjustment which had taken place between a couple. Husbands and wives were asked separately to select in order from a list of 30 automobile attributes, the five which they felt to be most important in making a realistic choice of a new family car. They were then asked to rank the 10 automobiles upon the basis of each of these selected attributes.

Discussion.—The conceptual framework presented suggests that viewing family purchase decision-making in the context of the goal-oriented behavior of a small group may be more satis-factory than examining it in terms of the relative power of husband and wife. It was found that the similarity between the husband's and wife's automobile preferences generally seems to be greater for families in the later stages of the family life cycle, as well as for families who have been married longer. Contrary to conventional views of the process of adjustment, there is a decline in agreement after 26 years of marriage as well as in the last two stages of the family life cycle.

The comparison of family life cycle and length of marriage indicated that the family life cycle is a superior explanatory variable and suggests that the process is not simply a function of time, but rather a function of the cumulative pressures toward goal-congruent behaviors. Further, the analysis tends to sug-gest that the presence of children is one of the principal pres-sures which tends to bring about this goal-congruent behavior. Families who do not have children and those who no longer have children at home are less likely to be goal congruent.

It can be argued that families do not increase in their degree of adjustment as they remain married. Rather, it may be that the increase in adjustment figures for families who had been mar-ried longer is an indication that the families who did not agree did not remain married. While this is an important distinction on a theoretical level, it is probably less important on a practical level. It is important when doing research on family decision-making to know whether the husband or wife or both are being interviewed and to know their stage in the family life cycle.

Family Buying Decisions: A Cross-cultural Perspective.— Donald J. Hempel's (1974) study presents cross-cultural comparisons of husband-wife interaction in specific house buying decisions. The findings indicate that perceived roles vary more by sex of the respondent and stage in the decision process than by the cultural content of the purchase.

Conceptual Approach and Method.—Husband-wife interaction in family decisions was measured with a series of questions about the relative importance of each spouse in specific decisions at different stages in the house buying process. Two different measures of husband-wife roles were contained in separate self administered questionnaires. The husband was asked to identify who was "mainly responsible" for selected decisions, while the wife was asked to indicate the "relative influence" of each spouse in these buying decisions.

An overall index of perceived dominance was computed for each spouse by adding the scores for five major purchase decisions concerning choice of neighborhood, style of house, when to buy, acceptable price and mortgage source. The data were obtained from a survey of recent home buyers conducted during the summer of 1968 and 1971. The first sample involved 206 families living near or in Hartford, Connecticut. The 1971 study included 317 households from seven towns in northwest England. Both investigations incorporated probability samples of households who purchased either a new or previously occupied house. Personal interviews were conducted with the husband and/or wife in the 523 sample households. The interviews were followed by two self-administered questionnaires.

Findings.—Who initiates the house-buying decision process? Previous studies indicate that joint decision-making is lower at this stage of the decision process, the husband playing the dominant role. This pattern was confirmed in Connecticut where husband-initiated moves exceeded shared decisions by a small margin. In northwest England more than half of the respondents identified this as a joint decision.

Purchase Decision Role.—Joint decision-making predominates in both cultures. Almost three of every four households reported that the neighborhood and style decisions were shared. Less than half of the families perceived the choice of mortgage source to be a shared decision. Both sexes perceived more sharing of decision roles in England than in Connecticut. The evidence suggests that some role specialization does exist in both countries. The wives concentrate on the social-expressive decisions and husbands are involved in the financial-instrumental decisions.

Sexual differences in role perceptions were greater than the international differences. Wives more than husbands perceived a joint role in all five purchase decisions, but the differences were greatest for decisions regarding mortgage source and style of house. Both spouses tended to perceive themselves as more influential than reported by their mates, especially for the mortgage decision. There was greater cultural similarity in the role performance reported by husbands than in that reported by wives. A chi-square test indicated no significant cultural differences for husbands. The decisions about when to buy, price and mortgage were much more likely to be reported as joint decisions by English wives.

Role Consensus.—The proportion of couples who agree on individual decisions is similar across cultures and decision areas. These role patterns indicate that house buying is a cooperative venture in which joint decision-making predominates. According to husbands' reports, his role was dominant in one of every three families. English wives were significantly less likely to perceive decision patterns dominated by the husband. The cultural differences in the role structure distributions were statistically significant for wives but not for husbands. The value of individual decisions as predictors of family role structure is greater for the instrumental decisions about when to purchase, price and mortgage.

Conflicts in Family Decisions.—Unresolved differences of opinion between husband and wife can delay the purchase and limit sales. If the areas of intrafamily conflict can be identified, then communications can help the couple to reach agreement or compromise. Knowledge which enables one to anticipate conflict areas can help to increase buyer satisfaction as well as market efficiency.

Discussion.—This investigation reveals a high degree of cross-cultural similarity in the household decision-making process. The differences between the roles perceived by husbands and wives within the same cultural setting were greater than the differences between cultures for either sex. The evidence supports the contention that accurate and reliable insights into family buying decisions cannot be obtained from responses of the husband or wife alone. If it is necessary to restrict inquiry to a single respondent, then variations in the extent of agreement across different market segments should be considered.

The relationship between intrafamily consensus and the demographic and life style characteristics of the household was examined. The findings indicate that the extent of husband-wife agreement in both cultures is related to family size, stage in life cycle, attitudes toward previous residence and life-style.

There is a tendency for the husband to be more involved than the wife as the initiator of the home-buying process. Husbands were more involved in decisions concerning the mortgage, price and when to buy, while wives were more involved in decisions regarding neighborhood and house style. These role distributions were similar in both cultures.

Perceived roles in the instrumental decisions (timing, price and mortgage) offered the most reliable base for inferences about the total decision patterns. Information about role allocations in the decision concerning when to buy appears to be the most useful single predictor of dominance in other purchase decisions.

Studies of house-buying decisions can contribute some unique insights into these role structures, because they represent a product class in which there is a very high interest and involvement of family members.

Conclusions.—The importance of the emerging female role in decision-making is brought out in the Green and Cunningham study. They do point out, however, that both husband and wife responses should be required for a valid and reliable indication of family decision-making patterns. Harry L. Davis (1971) writes that a multi-trait, multi-method approach for determining convergent and discriminant validity approach provides more information about the adequacy of influence measures than does a single trait or single rater approach. Davis states that there is evidence that the responses of husbands and wives are very similar when compared on an aggregate basis but dissimilar on a within-family basis. The largest discrepancies between husbands and wives seem to occur in their reports about decision-making.

Eli Cox has shown the importance of the family life cycle in decision-making. Whether or not there are children in the family tends to have an affect on the agreement of husbands and wives in decision-making.

The Hempel study also contends that accurate and reliable insights into family buying decisions must be obtained from responses of both husband and wife. He finds that husband-wife agreement is related to family size, stage in life cycle and life style.

The above studies show that the role of the emerging woman, family adjustment and stages in life cycle all affect purchasing decision-making and are important factors of the theory of buyer behavior.

REFERENCES

BARTOS, O. J. 1970. Determinants and consequences of toughness. *In* The Structure of Conflict. (P. Swingle, Editor.) Academic Press, New York.

BLAU, P. M. 1964. Exchange and Power in Social Life. John Wiley and Sons, New York.

COX, E. P., III. 1975. Family purchase decision making and the process of adjustment. J. Market. Res. *12*, 189–95.

DAVIS, H. L. 1971. Measurement of husband-wife influence in consumer purchase decisions. J. Market. Res. *8* (8) 205–212.

DRUCKMAN, D. 1967. Dogmatism, prenegotiation experience, and simulated group representation as determinants of dyadic behavior in a bargaining situation. J. Personality Soc. Psychol. *6*, 279–290.

DRUCKMAN, D. 1968. Prenegotiation experience and dyadic conflict resolution in a bargaining situation. J. Exper. Soc. Psychol. *4*, 367–383.

GARDNER, D. 1971. Can Bales' interaction process analysis be used to explore consumer behavior? *In* Consumer Behavior: Contemporary Research in Action. (Robert J. Holloway, Robert A. Mittelstaedt and M. Venkatesan, Editors.) Houghton Mifflin, Boston.

GREEN, R. T. and CUNNINGHAM, I. 1975. Feminine role perception and family purchasing decision. J. of Market. Res. *12*, 325–32.

HARSANYI, J. C. 1956. Approaches to the bargaining problem before and after the theory of games: A critical discussion of Zeuthen's, Hicks', and Nash's theories. Econometrica *24*, 144–157.

HEMPEL, D. J. 1974. Family buying decisions: A cross-cultural perspective. J. Market. Res. *11* (8) 295–302.

HOMANS, G. C. 1961. Social Behavior: Its Elementary Forms. Harcourt, Brace and World, New York.

KAHN, A. S. and KOHLS, J. W. 1972. Determinants of toughness in dyadic bargaining. Sociometry *35*, 305–315.

KASSARJIAN, H. and ROBERTSON, T. 1968. Perspectives in Consumer Behavior. Scott, Foreman, and Co., Glenview, Ill.

KELLEY, H. H. 1966. A classroom study of the dilemmas in interpersonal negotiations. *In* Strategic Interaction and Conflict. (K. Archibald, Editor.) Inst. for Int. Stud., Berkeley.

KELLEY, H. H., BECKMAN, L. L. and FISHER, C. S. 1967. Negotiating the division of a reward under incomplete information. J. of Exper. Soc. Psychol. *3*, 361–398.

KELLEY, H. H. and THIBAUT, J. W. 1969. Group problem solving. *In* Handbook of Social Psychology. 2nd edition, vol. 4. (G. Lindzey and E. Aronson, Editors.) Addison-Wesley, Reading, Mass.

KENKEL, W. F. 1957. Influence differentiation in family decision making. Sociol. Soc. Res., *42*.

KENKEL, W. F. 1961A. Dominance, persistence, self-confidence, and spousal roles in decision making. J. of Soc. Psychol., *54*.

KENKEL, W. F. 1961B. Husband-wife interaction in decision making and decision choice. J. Soc. Psychol., *54*.

KOMAROVSKY, M. 1961. Class differences in family decision making. *In* Consumer Behavior: Household Decision-making. (Nelson N. Foote, Editor.) New York Univ. Press, New York.

LIEBERT, R. M., SMITH, W. P., KEIFFER, M. and HILL, J. H. 1968. The effects of information and the magnitude of the initial offer on interpersonal negotiation. J. Exper. Soc. Psychol. 431–441.

NEWMAN, P. 1965. The Theory of Exchange. Prentice-Hall, Englewood Cliffs, N.J.

SHARP, H. and MOTT, P. 1956. Consumer decisions in the metropolitan family. J. Market. *21* (10) 149–156.

SIEGEL, S. and FOURAKER, L. E. 1960. Bargaining and Group Decision Making. McGraw-Hill, New York.

THIBAUT, J. W. and KELLEY, H. H. 1959. The Social Psychology of Groups. John Wiley and Sons, New York.

WALUM, L. 1977. The Dynamics of Sex and Gender: A Sociological Perspective. Rand McNally, Chicago.

9

General Laws Revisited

In the first chapter, four universal themes of human behavior were described: diminishing returns, utility maximization, organization and consistency, and desires as constraints on desires. Many theorists, working from very different perspectives, have made use of the same principles. One can now trace these themes through the various theories described.

Diminishing Returns.—As units of variable input (i.e., labor, time, goods consumed) increase with amounts of other (fixed) inputs held constant, output (production, performance, satisfaction) increases but at a decreasing rate.

Diminishing returns is most evident in economic theory. Diminishing marginal utility formed the core of marginal utility theory. A diminishing marginal rate of substitution becomes a key assumption in indifference curve analysis.

However, diminishing returns also becomes evident in a few other theories. A major implication of diminishing returns is that a person will diversify his/her activities or goods consumed, rather than continue along one avenue indefinitely. This diversification of activities occurs in motivation and personality theories. In particular, Maslow's hierarchy holds that a person will advance from one need to another as the former becomes largely chronically satisfied; this indicates that diminishing returns operates on the satisfaction from the fulfillment of the former need. The psychic energy system stated as a postulate that

energy moves from regions of greater to regions of lesser concentration; this again illustrates some sort of operation of diminishing returns.

Finally, human learning and physiological responses also follow patterns of diminishing returns with respect to time or
exertion. These findings in psychology, coupled with the theoretical developments noted above and the identical principle in
the economics of production, fairly firmly establish the idea of
diminishing returns as universal. While diminishing returns
itself comprises but a special case of the law of variable proportions (see Chapter 1), evidence as yet is insufficient to establish
the segments of increasing returns and decreasing product as
universal among the noneconomic social sciences.

Utility Maximization.—A person will seek to maximize his/
her satisfaction, subject to whatever constraints exist in the
situation.

The importance of utility maximization as the assumed motivation in economic theory need not be reemphasized. Less
obvious, perhaps, is the role of utility maximization in the other
types of theories.

One can think of hedonism, the basic assumption of learning
theory, as utility maximization. A person who seeks to gain
pleasure and avoid pain surely maximizes utility. Horney in her
personality theory holds that a person will select a strategy
based in part on what has given most satisfaction in the past and
in part on what is expected to give most satisfaction in the
current situation. The members of Cattell's group tend to choose
a leader who will help them maximize their own satisfaction.
Rogers' self-actualization suggests an implicit maximization of
satisfaction in the reinforcement of a given self-concept; this also
could result from the path of least effort.

The adjustment function of attitudes is by definition utility
maximization. Attitude change also involves maximization of
utility, but in another sense. The other side of maximization of
gain is the minimization of cost; the two approaches yield the
same result. The dissonance or tension arising from inconsistency is a cost. The attitude change theories hold that a person
will seek to minimize the dissonance and to do this with the least
effort possible. Therefore, attitude change theory also involves
the maximization of satisfaction.

Organization and Consistency.—The human mind has a strong need for organization and consistency.

This theme occurs in the assumptions on consumer preferences in indifference curve analysis. Preferences were assumed to be transitive, that is, if A is preferred to B and B to C, then A is preferred to C. This involves consistency of the ordering which of course is an organization of preferences. Maslow indirectly alluded to the need for this in his discussion of the need for safety.

The need for organization becomes most evident in all theories of perception. Chapter 3 dealt largely with this, so further elaboration here is unnecessary. The other most obvious example of a need for organization occurs in attitude theories.

The structural approach to attitudes in its definition of the subject considers an attitude as an organization of beliefs. Two of the functions described in the functional approach are knowledge and value-expression. The knowledge function restates the logic given by the perception theorists. The value-expressive function implies consistency between a person's values and attitudes. The literature on the relationship between attitudes and behavior deals with a presumed consistency between them. Under all theories of attitude change, a person attempts to achieve consistency among attitudes and between attitudes and behavior (for such would eliminate dissonance).

The self-concept theories depend on the individual's perceptions of him/herself and others. Since they follow the general laws of perception, they include the need for organization. Further, a person presumably behaves in accordance with his/her self-concept; this again implies consistency between self-concept, attitudes and behavior.

Other illustrations of organization and consistency occur in the conformity, social class and culture literature. A person in general will behave so as not to be too inconsistent with the surrounding society. Social behavior itself tends to be organized by means of norms, roles, etc.

Finally, consistency strongly contributes to the acquisition of patterns of behavior. Learning requires a consistency of patterns of stimuli and of response and reinforcement, in order to build up the requisite associations. Personality by definition is a fairly stable pattern; this also necessitates an organization to and consistency of the various behaviors.

Desires vs Constraints on Desires.—A person's behavior is determined by his/her resolution of the conflict between his/her desires and the constraints he/she faces.

This theme best translates as "you can't do everything you want." This appears to hold true in any context. Economic theory expresses it as the budget constraint on the individual's preferences. Perception involves both structural (physical/physiological) factors and functional (psychological) factors. In Maslow's hierarchy, the emergence and fulfillment of the higher order needs are constrained by lack of fulfillment of the lower order needs. Freud's id is constrained by the ego and superego. In the personality theories, but especially in symbolic interaction, other people must react to an individual's behavior and thus serve to constrain it. This also became evident in the conformity studies. Reinforcement, especially the negative variety, constrains behavior in learning theory, and other attitudes may constrain a given attitude (so as to induce or preserve consistency) in attitude change theories.

Thus, these themes appear widespread if not universal. The examples cited for each were meant to be illustrative rather than exhaustive, but sufficient evidence exists to assert that the themes exist across disciplines and may provide general laws for a unified social science.

Index

Acquisition, 97, 166
Actualization, 99-100
Adjustment function, 78, 218
Advertising, 62-65, 83-86, 108-115,
    142, 164-176
Aggression, 93-94, 105-107
Attention, 46, 48-52, 98
    allocation of processing resources,
        51-52
    necessity, 48-49
    selective perception, 46-47, 50- 51
    selective retention, 51
Attitudes, 12, 74-89, 91, 100-103,
        111, 141, 149-162, 220
    and behavior, 79-83, 219
    change, 77-79, 102-103, 149-157,
        176-179
    attribution theory, 162
    balance theory, 149-157, 176-179
        Heider, 149-151
        Rosenberg and Abelson, 151-
            157, 176-179
    congruity theory, 157-159
    dissonance theory, 159-162, 179-
        181, 218
    functional approach, 77-79, 102-
        103, 218-219
    information processing approach,
        79, 84-85
    structural approach, 75-77, 83, 219
    toward cereals, 83-86
    toward credit, 102-103
    toward object, 80-81, 178
    toward situation, 80-83, 102
Attribution theory, 162

Balance theory, 149-157, 176-179
    Heider, 149-151
    Rosenberg and Abelson, 151-157,
        176-179
Bandura, Albert, 96-99
Beliefs, 75-77
Bem, Daryl, 162
Biology, 60-61, 91-92
Brand loyalty, 114, 147, 162
Budget line, 12, 18-22, 42, 44, 54-57,
    74-75, 95, 131, 133, 155,
    220

Cattell, 61, 88-93, 95, 101-102, 122-
    124, 218
    personality theory, 88-93, 95, 101-
        102
    social group theory, 122-124, 218
Centrality, 76, 80
Ceteris paribus, 9
Children, 83-86, 97, 164-176, 201-
    202, 209-210
Choice, 21, 131, 220
Clothing, 103-107
Cognitive dissonance, 159-162, 179-
    181, 218
College decision, 176-179
Complementary goods, 35
Compliance, 93-94, 105-107
Conditioning, 146-148
Conditions of worth, 99
Conformity, 93, 127-129, 131, 219

Consistency, 11, 46, 99-100, 131, 134, 143, 149-162, 176, 219
Constraints, see Budget line
Contract curve, 187, 190, 199
Consumer credit, 37-42, 101-103
Cortical inhibition and excitation, 91-92
Cue, 95
Culture, 48, 132-134, 211-213, 219

Deductive logic, 4-5
Deferred gratification, 99, 131
Demand curve, 29-31, 33-35
Dependence, 192-194, 196, 199, 201
Desires vs constraints on desires, 12, 220
Detachment, 93-94, 105-107
Dieting, 137-143
Differentiation, 76, 99
Dimensions of attitudes, 76-77, 178
Diminishing returns, 11-12, 217-218
Discrimination, 148
Dissonance, 159-162, 179-181, 218
Dollard and Miller, 95
Drive, 95

Economic theory, 14-42, 185-191
  and social sciences, 6-7, 11, 43-44, 201
  assumptions, 14, 16
  exchange theory, 185-191
  income, changes in, 20, 23-26
    elasticity, 32
  indifference curve analysis, 12, 15-42, 217, 219
    budget lines, 18-22, 42, 44, 54-57, 74-75, 131, 133, 155, 220
    choice, 22, 39-40, 220
    consumer credit, 37-42
    elasticity, 29-34, 36-37, 148
  indifference curves, 16-18, 39-41, 83, 99, 185-196, 199, 220
  prices, changes in, 20, 26-35
    complementary goods, 34-35
    demand curve, 29-31, 33-35
    elasticity, 31-34, 36-37, 148

price consumption curve, 27-29
    substitute goods, 34-35
  marginal utility, 14-15
Ego-defensive function, 78, 102
Elasticity, 31-34, 36-37, 148
Engel curves, 24-26
Erg, 89-91, 101
Esteem needs, 59, 69-70
Exchange theory, 185-201
  economic framework, 185-191
    contract curves, 187, 190, 199
    offer curves, 187
  social psychology, 191, 201
    dependence, 192-194, 196, 199
    information, 197-198
    power, 189, 192-194, 196, 199
    risk, 198-199
    toughness, in bargaining, 196-199
Excitation, cortical, 91-92
Extroversion, 91-92
Eysenck, 91-93

Factor analysis, 89, 91, 122
Family, 129, 200-214
Freud, 60-61, 90, 93, 220
Functional approach to attitudes, 77-79, 102-103, 218-219
Functional determinants of perception, 45, 220
Function of groups, 126

Generalization, 148
General laws, 5, 9, 11-12, 217-220
  desires vs constraints, 12, 220
  diminishing returns, 11-12, 217-218
  organization and consistency, 11, 219
  utility maximization, 12, 14-15, 57, 78, 218
Genetics, 91-92
Groups, 121-134
  influence, 127-128, 140, 201
    Asch, 127-129
    conformity, 127-129, 219
  nature of, 121-127
    Cattell's approach, 122-124

function, 126
reference groups, 126-127, 139, 142
structure, 124-125
types of reference groups, 129-134
culture, 132-134, 219
family, 129, 200-214
social class, 129-131, 138, 219

Heider, 149-151
Horney, 93-94, 105-107
Hull, 61
Humanistic approach to personality, 99-100

Ideal types, 9
Income, 19-20, 23-26, 32, 56-57, 131, 155, 201, 203, 205
Indifference curve, 12, 16-18, 39-41, 83, 99, 185-196, 199, 217, 220
Inferior goods, 26, 32
Information, role in bargaining, 197-198
Information processing, 51-55, 79, 84-85, 98
Inhibition, cortical, 91-92
Interaction, social, 118-125, 132
Introversion, 91-92

Katz, 77-78, 102
Kinch, 120-121, 134-137
Knowledge function, 79, 102

Leader, group, 123-24
Learning, 74, 90, 95-99, 132-133, 140, 142, 145-148, 164-176, 218-220
acquisition vs perfomance, 97, 166
Bandura and Walters, 96-99
cue, 95
Dollard and Miller, 95-96
drive, 95

observational, 96-99, 131, 166-168
reinforcement, 94-98, 105, 132, 142, 146-147, 220
response, 95
social, 95-96
Long term memory, 53-54
Love needs, 59, 69-70

Marginal utility, 12, 14-15, 194, 217
Maslow, 12, 58-59, 69-71, 217, 220
Maximization of utility, 12, 14-15, 35, 57, 78, 218
Mead, 119
Memory, 52-55, 148
long term, 53-54
sensory store, 52-53
short term, 53
Mental set, 48, 49-50
Miller, 95-96
Mood, 48
Motivation, 12, 14, 57-62, 65-71, 95
actualization, 62
biological, 60-61
Cattell, 61, 218
Dollard and Miller, 61
Freud, 60-61, 90, 93, 220
Hull, 61
Maslow's hierarchy, 58-59, 69-71, 217, 220
Murray, 61
psychic energy, 56, 60-61, 217-218
self-actualization, 59, 62, 69-70, 99-100
social, 61
tension reduction, 12, 61-62
utility maximization, 12, 14-15, 35, 57, 78, 218
with respect to skateboarding, 67-68
with respect to vegetables, 69-71
Murray, 61

Needs, 11, 46-59, 69-71, 217
Neisser, 49-50, 163
Neoanalytical school, 93-94, 105-107
Neuroticism, 91-92
Normal goods, 23, 31

Observational learning, 96-99, 131,
    166-168
Offer curve, 187
Organismic valuing process, 99
Organization, 11, 46, 75-77, 79, 100,
    120, 134, 163, 219
Osgood and Tannenbaum, 157-159

Perception, 45-57, 62-65, 100, 112-
        114, 120-121, 130, 134,
        145, 163, 178, 219-220
    attention, 46, 48-52, 98
        allocation of processing re-
            sources, 51-52
        necessity of, 48-49
        selective perception, 40-51
        selective retention, 51
    change, 163
    cycle, 49-50, 163
    determinants, 46-51
        culture, 48
        mental set, 48-50
        mood, 48
        organization, 11, 46, 219
        selectivity, 11, 46-47, 50-51
        structural and functional, 45,
            220
    memory, 51-55, 148
        long term, 53-54
        sensory store, 51-53
        short term, 53
    of risk, 55, 66-67
    of shampoo, 62-65
    of women's roles, 108-115
Perceptual cycle, 49-50, 163
Performance of behavior, 97, 166
Personality, 12, 88-117, 122-124,
        198, 200, 218-220
    Cattell, 88-93, 95, 101-102, 122-
        124, 218
    Eysenck, 91-93
    Horney, 93-94, 105-107, 218
    observational learning,   96-99,
        131, 166-168
    Rogers, 99-100, 113, 118, 218-219
    social learning, 95-96
Pet purchase, 179-181
Physiological needs, 58, 69
Power, 192-194, 196, 199
Prediction, 5, 9

Preferences, 16-18, 21, 35, 74-75, 99-
    100, 131, 133-134, 148-
    149, 200-201, 219-220
Price-consumption curve, 27-29
Prices, 10, 15, 19-20, 26-37, 54-57,
    148, 189
Psychic energy, 56, 60-61, 217-218
Psychoticism, 91-92

Rationality, 9, 57
Records, 134-137
Reference groups, 126-137, 129-134,
    139, 142
Reinforcement, 94-98, 105, 132, 142,
    146-147, 219-220
Response, 95, 98, 120, 135-137, 146-
    148, 219
Response sets, 74, 88, 145
Risk, 55, 66-67, 131, 198-199
Rogers, 62, 99-100, 113, 118, 218-219
Rokeach, 75, 77, 80-82
Rosenberg and Abelson, 151-157,
    176-179

Safety needs, 59, 69
Selective perception, 11, 46-47, 50-
    51, 163
Self-actualization, 59, 61-66, 69-70,
    99-100
Self-concept, 99-100, 102, 112-114,
    118-121, 134-137, 140-
    142, 218-219
Self-image, 78, 93, 100, 102, 113,
    140-142
Self-sentiment, 90
Sensory store, 52-53
Sentiment, 90-91, 95, 101
Short term memory, 53
Situation, 21, 77, 80-83, 102, 121,
    134, 149, 159, 163, 178
Social class, 121-131, 138, 219
Social constraint, 81-83
Social influence, 118-143
Social involvement, 81-83
Socialization, 132
Social learning, 95-96
Social motivation, 61

Social orientation, 93-94, 105-107
Social psychological exchange theory, 191-201
Social science, nature of, 6-8
   an inexact science, 6-7
   nature of theories in, 8-9
   relationship among social sciences, 43-44
   relationship between individual and society, 7-8

Stability, 81
Stimulus, 95, 146, 165, 219
Structural determinants of perception, 45, 220
Structure of attitudes, 75-77, 83, 219
Structure of groups, 124-125
Substitute goods, 34, 36-37
Superior goods, 24, 32
Symbolic interaction, 118-121, 134-137, 220
   and purchase of records, 134-137
   Kinch, 120-121, 134-137
   Mead, 119
Synergy, 122-123
Syntality, 122-124

Tension reduction, 12, 61-62, 149, 162
Testability, 4, 6, 9-11
Theory, and explanation, 2, 4-6, 8-9
   construction, 2-4
   deductive logic, 4-5
   general laws, 5, 9, 11-12, 217-220
   ideal types, 9
   limits in social science, 8-9
   nature of, 2-11
   prediction, 5, 9
   testability, 4, 6, 9-11
Toughness in bargaining, 196-199
Traits, 88-90, 93, 95, 101

Utility maximization, 12, 14-15, 35, 57, 78, 218

Value-expressive function, 78, 102
Verbal attitude, 81

Warner, 129-130
Women's roles, 84, 108-115, 200-214

Other AVI Books

DIETARY NUTRIENT GUIDE
Pennington
ECONOMICS OF FOOD PROCESSING
Greig
ECONOMICS OF NEW FOOD PRODUCT DEVELOPMENT
Desrosier and Desrosier
FOOD AND ECONOMICS
Hungate and Sherman
FOOD FOR THOUGHT
2nd Edition   *Labuza and Sloan*
FOOD SERVICE FACILITIES PLANNING
Kazarian
FOOD SERVICE SCIENCE
Smith and Minor
MENU PLANNING
2nd edition   *Eckstein*
NUTRITIONAL QUALITY INDEX OF FOODS
Hansen, Wyse and Sorenson
PACKAGING REGULATIONS
Sacharow
QUALITY CONTROL IN FOOD SERVICE
Thorner and Manning
SCHOOL FOODSERVICE
Van Egmond
WORK ANALYSIS AND DESIGN FOR HOTELS, RESTAURANTS
& INSTITUTIONS, 2nd Edition   *Kazarian*